CSR in the Middle East

Also by Dima Jamali and Yusuf Sidani

MANAGEMENT: ARAB WORLD EDITION (*co-edited with S.P. Robbins and M. Coulter*)

CSR in the Middle East

Fresh Perspectives

Edited by

Dima Jamali and Yusuf Sidani
American University of Beirut

palgrave
macmillan

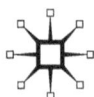

Selection and editorial content © Dima Jamali and Yusuf Sidani 2012
Individual chapters © the contributors 2012

All rights reserved. No reproduction, copy or transmission of this
publication may be made without written permission.

No portion of this publication may be reproduced, copied or transmitted
save with written permission or in accordance with the provisions of the
Copyright, Designs and Patents Act 1988, or under the terms of any licence
permitting limited copying issued by the Copyright Licensing Agency,
Saffron House, 6–10 Kirby Street, London EC1N 8TS.

Any person who does any unauthorized act in relation to this publication
may be liable to criminal prosecution and civil claims for damages.

The authors have asserted their rights to be identified as the authors of this
work in accordance with the Copyright, Designs and Patents Act 1988.

First published 2012 by
PALGRAVE MACMILLAN

Palgrave Macmillan in the UK is an imprint of Macmillan Publishers Limited,
registered in England, company number 785998, of Houndmills, Basingstoke,
Hampshire RG21 6XS.

Palgrave Macmillan in the US is a division of St Martin's Press LLC,
175 Fifth Avenue, New York, NY 10010.

Palgrave Macmillan is the global academic imprint of the above companies
and has companies and representatives throughout the world.

Palgrave® and Macmillan® are registered trademarks in the United States,
the United Kingdom, Europe and other countries.

ISBN 978–0–230–34821–9

This book is printed on paper suitable for recycling and made from fully
managed and sustained forest sources. Logging, pulping and manufacturing
processes are expected to conform to the environmental regulations of the
country of origin.

A catalogue record for this book is available from the British Library.

A catalog record for this book is available from the Library of Congress.

10   9   8   7   6   5   4   3   2   1
21 20 19 18 17 16 15 14 13 12

Printed and bound in Great Britain by
CPI Antony Rowe, Chippenham and Eastbourne

This book is dedicated to our fellow citizens
of the Middle East, with the hope that it will inspire
further engagement in corporate social responsibility
here and abroad

Contents

Illustrations

Tables

Figures

Boxes

Acknowledgments

We have been reflecting for some time on preparing a volume describing the evolution and dynamics of corporate social responsibility (CSR) in the Middle East, given the scarce knowledge base pertaining to this topic. After much reflection and introspection, we decided to embark on the journey of compiling a book that provides a better understanding of CSR and its peculiarities and manifestations across the region. However, this effort would not have been possible had it not been for Palgrave Macmillan's keen interest in the topic, and the positive and continuous reinforcement and support provided by Virginia Thorp and her team.

We sincerely thank the World Health Organization, the World Business Council for Sustainable Development, the SMAP Clearing House, the Prince's Accounting for Sustainability Project, the Institute of Chartered Accountants in England and Wales, and the Institute for Behavioral and Applied Management for their permission to reproduce certain tables and figures in this book. Their cooperation has enabled us to build and expand upon leading knowledge in the area of CSR.

The book has also benefited from the support of colleagues and friends at the American University of Beirut. To start with, we would like to express our most sincere thanks and gratitude to our graduate student, Charissa Lloyd, who has been helping us in this project from day one. Her meticulous and professional assistance every step of the way has not gone unnoticed, and she deserves praise and appreciation for that. We should also acknowledge the help of our other graduate students, particularly Liya Kreidie and Amy Walburn, who have been very vigilant and involved in editing and formatting issues in the various phases of the compilation of this project. We owe a debt of gratitude for their gracious help and support.

As with any edited volume, the most sincere thanks are extended to the authors of the chapters. We have been fortunate to work with a very committed selection of authors from countries across the Middle

East, including Jordan, the UAE, Egypt and Lebanon. They have been generous with their time and effort, not only providing interesting and relevant material, but also revising and re-drafting their respective chapters in response to numerous reviewer comments. They have shown an unwavering commitment to see the book through to completion and to the cause of advancing knowledge in this important area of research. Without their commitment and perseverance, this book would certainly not have been possible.

Contributors

Malyuba Abu-Daabes is assistant professor at the German Jordanian University. She obtained a BSc in chemical engineering from the University of Jordan in 1998 and a PhD in chemical engineering from the University of Cincinnati, USA, in 2005. Her core research competencies are in the architecture of advanced nano-structured materials for adsorption in environmental applications, trace metal speciation in air pollution, adsorption fundamentals and separation, and membrane separation and desalination.

Akram Al Ariss is a professor of human resource management at Toulouse Business School. He is also a visiting professor at the London School of Economics and is affiliated with Pennsylvania State University, where he lectures on international human resources management (IHRM) and employment relations. He holds a PhD from Norwich Business School, University of East Anglia, UK. Akram is interested in researching and teaching IHRM and has written book chapters, journal articles and book reviews on HRM in journals such as *Academy of Management Learning and Education* and *British Journal of Management*. He is the co-author (with Dessler) of the textbook *Human Resource Management, Arab World Edition*. He serves on the editorial boards of *Journal of World Business* and *Equality, Diversity, and Inclusion*.

Akram has experience in management consultancy and training in multinational organizations across Europe and the Arab region. He has consulted for organizations including Projacs (Arab Middle East), Alcatel (Paris), Assad Said Corporation (Kingdom of Saudi Arabia), RATP (Paris) and the Federal Demographic Council (United Arab Emirates). He was head of the HRM Department at Champagne School of Management (France) for three years until early 2012. He was also a visiting researcher at Brunel Business School in London in 2011.

Joseph Antoun is the President and CEO of Health System Reform SAL, a boutique advisory aimed at improving public health through health policy and health system management; the Co-director of the Center for Health Policy at the University of Chicago, where he teaches Health Systems and Pharmaceutical Policy; a professor of health policy at the Buck Institute in California; and a visiting fellow at the Department of Social Policy at the London School of Economics and Political Science. He has a master's in public policy from Harvard University and has completed health system financing and management studies at Johns Hopkins University. He obtained his doctorate in medicine and master's in medical and biological sciences at Saint Joseph University. His recent work, teaching and publications focus on health systems and systems reform, on leadership and new public management in healthcare, on rewarding healthcare innovation and on increasing access to medicines.

Tonnie Choueiri is currently Outreach Coordinator of the American University of Beirut (AUB) Neighborhood Initiative. She has an MSc in development studies from Copenhagen Business School and has worked in non-governmental organizations as well as private and educational institutions, in Denmark and Lebanon. Her main interests are in social, economic and community development.

Marian Eabrasu is a professor at the Champagne School of Management, Troyes, France, where he teaches ethics and economics. He has previously been an assistant professor at the Paris VIII University (Saint-Denis, France), and a research fellow at the International Centre for Economic Research (Turin, Italy). His research interests cover three main areas: corporate social responsibility (good practices in CSR, ISO 26000, tax evasion), moral philosophy (theories of justice, libertarianism), and economic theory and policy (subjective theory of value, normative economics). The results of his research are available in several international peer-reviewed journals and book chapters. In 2011, he co-authored an article entitled 'The Ethics of Tax Evasion', published in the *Business and Society Review* (vol. 116, no. 3, pp. 375–401); he is the author of a book chapter entitled 'Towards a Convergence of the Ethics of Tax Evasion and Secession' in Robert McGee (ed.), *The Ethics of Tax Evasion in Theory and Practice* (pp. 107–125); and he received the prize for the best developmental paper in CSR at the 25th conference of the British Academy of Management, for the paper: 'A Moral Pluralism Perspective on Corporate Social Responsibility'.

Aida El-Khatib currently works as a laboratory teaching assistant at the American University of Sharjah, UAE, and is in the process of attaining her MBA. She is interested in sustainability and its role in transforming business models. She holds a BBA with a concentration in accounting and finance. Her past engagements include working as an assistant relationship manager at a Standard Chartered Bank branch in the UAE, as well as working as an analyst on real-estate projects in the UAE.

David L. Haskell serves as founding President and CEO of Dreams InDeed, an international development network that strengthens indigenous social entrepreneurs in hard places to enable the poor to thrive. He has three decades of experience ranging from blended value business to venture philanthropy, launching six successful Middle Eastern start-ups and directing four East African turnarounds. As the founding Regional Director of Habitat for Humanity in the Middle East and East Africa, he doubled its impact to 2400 families housed a year. A Harvard Pforzheimer Fellow and University of Jordan Fulbright Scholar, David received an Outstanding Teaching Award from UCLA. He has presented at the business or graduate schools of AUB, Adelphi, UC Berkeley, Harvard, Notre Dame, Oxford, Princeton, Stanford, Tufts and Wheaton. He also co-authored *Spiritual Resources for Change in Hard Places: A Values-Driven Social Entrepreneurship Theory of Change* (2009). David earned his master's in public administration from Harvard, specializing in leadership, negotiation, mediation and conflict resolution; his master's in applied linguistics from UCLA; and his BA in communications *magna cum laude* from Wheaton.

Janice Hayashi Haskell serves as founding Vice-President for Program Development at Dreams InDeed, an international development network that strengthens indigenous social entrepreneurs in hard places to enable the poor to thrive. She weaves values-aligned networks, fosters social innovation and applies adaptive evaluation approaches to strengthen indigenous social entrepreneurs. Currently at work in challenging pockets of the Arab World and South-east Asia, she has 30 years of experience in social development and leadership coaching in the Middle East, Africa, Asia and the USA. Janice co-authored *Spiritual Resources for Change in Hard Places: A Values-Driven Social Entrepreneurship Theory of Change* (2009) and authored *Globalization and Migration: the Perspective of the Child* (1997). She earned her master's in international affairs from Tufts Fletcher School of Law and Diplomacy; her master's in education *summa cum laude* from Portland State University; and her BA in psychology *cum laude* from Lewis and Clark.

Muna Y. Hindiyeh obtained her PhD in environmental engineering from Newcastle University, UK, in 1995. She has more than 20 years of experience in water and wastewater microbiology and environmental health. She received the Arab Award for the Sheikh Abdallah Al-Mubark Al-Subah for Scientific Research at the second level for the Arab World Level. She was appointed as assistant professor at the Environmental and Water Engineering Department of the German Jordanian University in 2008. Muna has much experience in social and environmental responsibility and was appointed Head of the National Mirror Committee regarding social responsibility guideline ISO 26000. She has conducted training courses, organized conferences, and been a keynote speaker on social and environmental responsibility at many conferences in the region, and issued a report entitled 'Corporate Environmental Responsibility in Jordan' supported by the United Nations Development Programme. She had been a board member of the Jordanian Institution for Standardisation and Meteorology, Jordanian Sustainable Development Society, Friends of Earth Society, Darat Shama for Elderly People and the Cultural Youth and Children Society, and she is also founder of the International Alliance for Women and Water and the National Environmental Media Society. She has participated in many national committees, such as the Lower House of Parliament, National Health Strategy and Environmental National Information, in addition to the Water Consumption Reduction Concept Committee for national school curriculums and Water Safety Plan. She has been a member in the Arab Family committee at the Arab Countries League. She also serves with national and international development organizations, such as the World Health Organization, UNDP and the US Agency for International Development (USAID).

Dima Jamali is a professor in the School of Business at AUB and chair of the Management, Marketing and Entrepreneurship Track. She holds a PhD in social policy and administration from the University of Kent at Canterbury, UK. Her research/teaching revolves primarily around CSR. She is the author of more than 40 international publications focusing on different aspects of CSR in the Middle East, all appearing in highly reputable journals, including *British Journal of Management, Corporate Governance: An International Review, Journal of Business Ethics* and *Business Process Management*. Her research record has won her a number of scientific awards and honors, including the Abdul Hameed Shoman Award for Best Young Arab Researcher for the year 2010, Best Paper Awards at the Irish Academy of Management (2011) and the American Academy of Management (2008), British Academy of Management Fellowship for South Asia and Middle East (2007), and the Best Paper Award by the North American Case Research Association (2003). She has worked as an expert consultant for the United Nations on social policy and CSR as well as various projects funded by the World Bank, USAID, NGOs and other local public and private firms.

Sari Kassis is a trade unionist who is working hard to spread the practice of collective bargaining to any and all businesses or organizations he works with or happens to pass. While he works to organize workers into reclaiming their workplace, he also serves as a director on the board of Locrete Holdings Limited, a Palestinian company with a patented low-cost building system, and he is working on the expansion of Q perspective – a specialized consulting firm that offers, among other things, comprehensive CSR solutions to corporations – into the Lebanese market. Sari is currently putting his studies in political economics at the University of Sydney to good use by getting involved in projects that join together social and political activism with sustainable, long-term plans to try to change the world for the better at the expense of those who can afford it and in favor of those who need it.

Yazan Majaj is an expert in sustainable human development with more than ten years' experience in designing and implementing CSR programs and activities in Jordan and the Middle East. Having worked in the private sector immediately after graduating from AUB in 2000, he moved to the regional office of the United Nations Development Fund for Women (previously UNIFEM, now UN Women) as a project manager for Economic Empowerment Projects until he eventually came to manage the regional Economic Security and ICT Programme in the Arab Region. In 2008, he and several of his team left UNIFEM and started Q perspective, a specialized consulting firm that offers comprehensive CSR solutions to corporations as part of its services. Since then, the company has designed and managed CSR, social investment and philanthropic projects and programs for leading companies in Jordan. Majaj dedicates time and effort to voluntary work and serves as a consultant, pro bono, for several NGOs based in Jordan. He is a strong advocate of food security, employability and educational efforts directed in underprivileged communities of youth, refugees and women. He graduated from AUB with a degree in psychology and completed his master's in international business at the New York Institute of Technology through a program offered through the Jordan University of Science and Technology.

Cynthia Myntti is a professor of public health practice at AUB. She received her MA in anthropology from AUB in 1974, before going on to do a PhD in social anthropology at the London School of Economics (1983) and a master's in public health from Johns Hopkins University (1986). She worked as a program officer in the Ford Foundation offices in Cairo and Jakarta for nearly a decade, and held teaching positions at Sanaa University in Yemen, the London School of Hygiene and Tropical Medicine and the University of Minnesota in the USA. In 1998 she returned to AUB as a visiting associate professor in the Faculty of Health Sciences. After publishing *Paris along the Nile: Architecture in Cairo from the Belle Epoque* (1999) she decided to return to graduate school, in architecture, graduating with an M Arch from Yale in 2004. Since 2006 she has directed the Neighborhood Initiative at AUB.

Jessica Jinju Pottenger provides executive support for the Middle East regional office of Dreams InDeed, an international development network that strengthens indigenous social entrepreneurs in hard places to enable the poor to thrive. She supports program development, designs management information systems, develops training materials, and coordinates international communications and social media networks. She previously served in China and North Korea as an editor for the NGO Citizens' Alliance for North Korean Human Rights, publishing the briefing reports 'Homecoming Kinsmen or Indigenous Foreigners?', 'The Case of North Korean Re-settlers in South Korea', 'The Battered Wheel of the Republic: NKHR Briefing Report on Violence against Women in North Korea' and 'Flowers, Guns, and Women on Bikes: NKHR Briefing Report on the Situation of Women's Rights in the DPRK'. Jessica earned her BA *magna cum laude* from the Woodrow Wilson School of Public and International Affairs at Princeton University.

Haitham E. Salti holds a BSc in chemical-pharmaceutical engineering from the German Jordanian University, 2010. He started his career at Arab Pharmaceutical Manufacturing (Hikma PLC) by co-initiating a project that tackled corporate environmental responsibility in the Jordanian pharmaceutical industry through applying the cleaner production approach. This study, which was the first of its kind in the region, resulted in identifying several environmentally friendly options for both case companies, thereby contributing to significant savings. He led the 'Lean Manufacturing' initiative, which focuses on eliminating waste through creating standardized processes requiring less human effort, less capital and less time to make products at a lower cost and with much fewer defects. He recently joined the MENA Process Improvement & Technology Transfer Department at Hikma Corporate.

Yusuf Sidani is an Associate Professor of Management at the Suliman Olayan School of Business at the American University of Beirut. His articles appeared in such journals as the *Journal of Business Ethics, Journal of Social Psychology, Business and Society Review* and *Gender in Management: An International Journal*.

Alexandra Tarazi graduated with a BA in political science from AUB in 2007. She then decided to pursue a career in the non-profit sector, working in several NGOs abroad and in Lebanon on issues as diverse as children's rights, environmental awareness and women's empowerment. In 2012 she received an MA in Applied human rights from the University of York, with a dissertation on corporate responsibility in SMEs in Lebanon. Upon graduation, she continued her academic journey, working as a research assistant for AUB's CSR initiative on the evolution of CSR and social entrepreneurship in countries across the Middle East.

Jeannette Vinke is a senior lecturer at the American University of Sharjah. She is interested in sustainability and integrated reporting by research, training and consulting. She is currently researching the state of integrated reporting in the Gulf Cooperation Council. Jeannette is an advisory board member of the Institute of Chartered Accountants in England and Wales. Her past engagements at Deutsche Bank included leading the Cash Equities Finance team for Germany, and later, as CFO for MENA, she was one of the bank's architects in entering the region, with responsibility for setting up entities in Dubai, Abu Dhabi, Riyadh, Bahrain, Algiers, Cairo and Qatar. She has also held senior positions with KPMG in Europe and the Middle East, dealing with a variety of industries. Her portfolio in the Middle East included HSBC, Commercial Bank of Dubai and Panasonic. Her SME activities include organizing and negotiating a buyout of the Dubai-based company AME Info as the company's CFO.

Abbreviations and Acronyms

A4S	Accounting for Sustainability
AARP	American Association of Retired Persons
API	active pharmaceutical ingredient
ATM	access to medicines
AUB	American University of Beirut
CAS	Central Administration of Statistics
CCECS	Center for Civic Engagement and Community Service
CDP	chronic diseases partnerships
CER	corporate environmental responsibility
CP	clean production
CSR	corporate social responsibility
DFID	Department for International Development
EDL	essential drug list
EIA	Environmental Impact Assessment
EPA	Environmental Protection Agency
ESCWA	United Nations Economic and Social Commission for Western Asia
ESG	Environmental, Social and Governance
GC	Global Compact
GCC	Gulf Cooperation Council
GRI	Global Reporting Initiative
GSK	GlaxoSmithKline
HIV/AIDS	Human Immunodeficiency Virus/Acquired Immune Deficiency Syndrome
HRM	human resource management
ICAEW	Institute of Chartered Accountants in England and Wales
IDF	International Diabetes Foundation
IFC	International Finance Corporation
INSEAD	Institut Européen d'Administration des Affaires
IPIECA	International Petroleum Industry Environmental Conservation Association
IRP	international reference pricing

ISO	International Standard Organization
ITI	International Trachoma Initiative
JAPM	Jordanian Association of Pharmaceutical Manufacturers
JCPP	Jordan Clean Production Program
JD	Jordanian Dinar
JNEFI	Jordanian Network for Environmentally Friendly Industries
KKRCA	King Khalid Responsible Competitiveness Award
KPI	Key performance indicator
LDC	least developed country
MDG	Millennium Development Goals
MDR-TB	multi-drug-resistant tuberculosis
MENA	Middle East and North Africa
MNC	multinational corporation
NCD	non-communicable disease
NGO	non-governmental organization
PRS	Pearl Rating System
R&D	research and development
SAGIA	Saudi Arabian General Investment Authority
SMEs	small and medium enterprises
TDS	total dissolved solids
UNDP	United Nations Development Programme
UNEP	United Nations Environment Program
UNIDO	United Nations Industrial Development Organization
VC	values curriculum
WBCSD	World Business Council for Sustainable Development
WHO	World Health Organization

Introduction: CSR in the Middle East: Fresh Perspectives

Dima Jamali and Yusuf Sidani

To date, the concept of corporate social responsibility (CSR) has not received systematic attention in the Middle East. Our excursion in this book is intended to flesh out the understanding and practice of CSR in this part of the world. As will be revealed through the various contributions, CSR in the Middle East has distinctive roots and unique expressions that do not always mirror the current understanding and practice in the West. Nevertheless, from the contributions that follow, the reader will be reassured to learn that CSR is alive and well in the Middle East, although it continues to have its unique flavor and connotations. Moreover, the group of scholars and practitioners that we have had the fortune to work with through the compiling of this book attest to an unwavering commitment to the basic concepts of collective effort and giving that are captured in the noble notion of CSR.

The contributors to this book have aptly pointed out that CSR in the Middle East builds on deeply rooted traditions of philanthropic giving that are deeply engrained across the region. Derived from the composite Greek words *phillen* (love) and *anthropos* (human), philanthropy in the Arab region continues to be rooted in strong religious and cultural traditions and in broad social values of empathy or compassion for fellow human beings. Giving and helping continue to have positive connotations across the region, and there is a proliferation of Arabic terms to express different forms of giving, including *zakat* (obligatory giving and one of the five pillars of the Islamic faith), *mabarra* (benevolent work), and *takaful insani* (humanitarian giving). These are inspired by various Islamic principles, such as

1

unity, justice, balance, trusteeship and benevolence, and from the basic concepts and tenets of the Islamic religion. In other words, Islamic philanthropy provides a strong foundation for CSR in the region, and constitutes a pivotal tradition of voluntary giving that falls outside the realm of presumed Western largesse.

The contributions to this book, however, have also highlighted the dynamics of change across the region and how the traditional forms of Islamic philanthropy are starting to cross-fertilize with new, more institutionalized, forms of giving advocated through Western concepts and advances pertaining to CSR. The unfolding of these change dynamics will be very interesting to observe as the region moves forward beyond the Arab Spring, and new collective institutions are built that preserve the sanctity of freedom, democracy and human rights. There is certainly room and a need in this newly reconfigured institutional space to leverage Islamic philanthropy and institutionalize it into more strategic forms of giving. This will ensure a more effective channeling of resources to serve the greater public good through addressing regional social ills and problems pertaining to economic development, unemployment, environmental protection, poverty alleviation, healthcare, education, community capacity building, human rights and the empowerment of women, among others.

Indeed, it could very well be argued that both philanthropy and CSR are more needed than ever before in the Arab region in view of the scope of challenges associated with the current financial crisis. Financial volatility and fluctuations in economic markets, coupled with dwindling government resources, are likely to take their toll on the quality of life and the well-being of future generations across the globe. Like its counterpart developed economies, the Middle East is grappling with the losing battle of sustainable development and with the social strains produced by these upheavals, which continue to be endemic and protracted globally, such as alleviating poverty, improving access to healthcare and education, and slowing down the degradation of biodiversity and loss of natural resources. Arab countries face, in this respect, the uncontested reality that markets must be embedded in broader frameworks of social value creation if they are to thrive and survive and that the corporate sector can advance this cause by embracing the universal values and concerns that lie at the heart of the notion of CSR.

Across the Middle East, philanthropic practices and entrenched forms of indigenous giving have no doubt been crucial to date in alleviating deep-seated social problems. However, with the blowing winds of change, what is needed in the Middle East at this critical juncture is a more institutionalized form of modern philanthropy that preserves the original social values but mobilizes resources more effectively in facilitating social change and promoting sustainable development. Strategic philanthropy requires a more careful scrutiny of resource allocation decisions, a systematic consideration of the social issues to address, a delicate selection of partners and granting conditions, as well as a proactive assessment of social impact or social returns. While it equally leverages the values of compassion and ethical leadership, it requires adjustments in how organizations approach their giving, with a focus on institutionalization, integration and outcome assessment. In other words, what is needed is to take existing philanthropy in the Arab world to the next level in terms of greater institutionalization, reporting and sophistication.

Islamic philanthropy, strategic philanthropy and CSR are therefore important trends for the region going forward. They are likely to ensure that the private sector is engaged, as it should be, as a vital partner in development through a responsible business framework. What the region also needs is to mobilize different forms of partnership or cross-sector collaboration to address common and complex social challenges or meta-social issues (e.g. clean water, clean air, environmental protection, healthcare and education), which are seen to have spillover effects on multiple constituencies and multiple stakeholders, yet transcend the boundaries or lie beyond the scope or capacity of a particular or single sector or organization. These new emergent forms of partnership that cross-fertilize the efforts of private, public and non-governmental partners are a pressing imperative for the region at this critical juncture, and will certainly be beneficial in taking CSR in the Middle East forward to the next level of institutionalization, enactment, monitoring and evaluation.

About the contributions to this book

It is clear from the above that CSR in the Middle East does not exactly fit or mirror the Western frame of analysis, and that CSR per se (in contrast with more traditional philanthropy) is still an emerging concept that requires further systematic attention and consideration. To sharpen our understanding of CSR in the Middle East, this volume draws on the experiences of practitioners and scholars who are currently living and working across the Middle East. Each author provides insights into an important aspect of CSR from their own unique vantage point or experience. Together, their contributions provide a more rounded understanding of CSR in the Middle East, its important distinctions and peculiarities, and strategic priorities for the future. The paragraphs below provide a brief summary, or the main highlights, for each of the eight contributions to this volume.

CSR and philanthropy: different forms of effective social investment

The distinction between philanthropy and CSR continues to galvanize global attention and perplex even the most sophisticated scholars. As outlined above, Islamic philanthropy is likely to provide a strong foundation for CSR in the region. In Chapter 1, Yazan Majaj and Sari Kassis dwell on these two forms of giving, or what they call 'social investment', and their expressions in the Middle East. They argue that traditional forms of giving, such as *zakat*, *sadaqa*, *waqf*, and direct charitable contributions are all expressions of mandated social responsibility in Islam that have enjoyed temporal consistency and are likely to facilitate the integration and consolidation of CSR. They also argue that through a process of mimetic isomorphism and the transfer of best practice from large multinational corporations, existing philanthropy in the region is likely to metamorphose with time into more strategic forms of giving/coordinated CSR programs governed by structured policies and institutions. They provide concrete examples of two local corporations, the Nuqul Group and Abdali PSC, and one subsidiary of a multinational corporation in Jordan, that have made significant strides in relation to both philanthropy and CSR, and managed to recognize and leverage the value of these two forms of social investment by pursuing two parallel tracks of corporate philanthropy and CSR. Hence, they conclude that while CSR is a welcome new trend, it is not a substitute, but rather a complement to the more entrenched version of philanthropic giving and traditions that have long permeated the Middle East region.

Harnessing values for impact beyond profit in the Middle East and North Africa

Opportunities for social entrepreneurship across the Middle East remain poorly explored, despite their great potential in relation to human development and social impact. Social entrepreneurship constitutes a peculiar expression of CSR, whereby an organization places a social mission at the center of its existence, prioritizing it over all aspects of its operations, even profits. In Chapter 2, David Haskell, Janice Haskell and Jessica Jinju Pottenger provide the powerful example of an innovative Egyptian social enterprise, Care with Love, which has managed, through the consistent refinement and practice of values, to have a profound social impact and fill important social gaps pertaining to unemployment and dedicated healthcare support for the housebound elderly and chronically ill. The distinctive feature of this social entrepreneurial organization is its peculiar approach to incorporating culturally rooted, spiritually inspired internal values into the process. Through a participatory process, employees jointly crafted a set of common values pertaining to faithfulness and integrity, humility, respect, commitment, teamwork, acceptance of others and sacrificial love to guide their practice in the social domain. The practice and enactment of these values translated into a profound social impact, as demonstrated through the social footprint of Care with Love, with the graduation of 924 caregivers in 14 years – most of whom are drawn from the marginalized unemployed segment of the population – and serving in the process 1450 elderly and ill clients within their own homes. The highlight of this chapter, however, is its poignant illustration, through the touching words of the caregivers themselves, of the profound social impact of Care with Love, which has improved the health of and respect for elders, sustained families, provided effective education and dignified employment, and improved inter-sectarian understanding; all of which have transformed the lives of the caregivers and their clients.

CSR to increase access to medicines: lessons and opportunities for the Middle East

Improved access to medicines is a crucial social issue which has not received enough attention in the Middle East. According to

Joseph Antoun, the author of Chapter 3, improving access to existing medicines could save 10 million lives each year worldwide. Unfortunately, however, there are no published data to quantify the impact of this in the Middle East context, despite the potentially significant implications for health outcomes and lifespan across the region. Antoun aptly points out that the issue of access to medicines is an important human right and a developmental challenge for the region going forward, and that the business sector has a responsibility in this respect to partner with patients and healthcare providers to increase access to medicines. Antoun highlights the main access to medicine challenges across the region, including the relatively high prices of non-reimbursed medicines despite low purchasing power and protracted per capita growth. He also fleshes out different CSR initiatives that could increase access to medicines in the Middle East. These include the traditional charitable donation of medicines which continue to be prevalent in the region but have a modest impact on public health in view of their scale and costs, but also a portfolio of other innovative CSR activities that are likely to increase access to medicines in a sustainable way, including: technology transfers, tiered pricing, dual branding, patient pharmaceutical cards, co-pay or co-insurance rebates, chronic disease partnerships and non-profit pharmaceuticals. These novel CSR interventions, he concludes, can go a long way in luring business interest, alleviating costs and increasing access to medicines in a sustainable manner, translating into positive win-win impacts and added value for businesses and the wider public health.

CSR: a cost or an opportunity for small and medium enterprises in the Middle East

Small and medium enterprises (SMEs) are internationally recognized as the seedbed for innovation in niche markets, risk-taking behavior and long-term economic growth and social stability. However, the knowledge base on CSR in SMEs in the Middle East is virtually non-existent, even though SMEs and family firms constitute an important backbone of the Middle East and North Africa regional economy, accounting for 75 per cent of the private sector economy and employing 70 per cent of the labor force. In Chapter 4, Dima Jamali and Alexandra Tarazi revisit the peculiar drivers, challenges and opportunities characterizing the engagement of SMEs in CSR across the Middle East. Using two case examples of SMEs from Lebanon, their findings confirm the close entangling of the personal and the social in the CSR practiced by SMEs, the strong influence of founders/owners, the flexibility in relation to decision-making and the greater sense of embeddedness within communities, which all provide an important roadmap for SMEs in the CSR domain. SMEs, they report, seem to have a spontaneous affinity with CSR, and their CSR seems grounded in a crystallized ethos system and values pertaining to trust, humanity and integrity. SMEs also focus their CSR practice on the vexing social issues lying at the heart of their community, as in elderly care, for example, or improved education and educational opportunities. In other words, their approach to CSR is more customized (less generic) than large businesses, and they exert consistent efforts both internally and externally to refine their choices of causes and interventions that would add value to their internal and external stakeholders. The most interesting highlight of this chapter is the authors' conclusion that SMEs need not look at CSR as a cost, but rather as an opportunity for engagement, innovation and differentiation, and that even in a difficult business environment, and with limited resources, SMEs can identify a path to make a positive difference in the lives of their employees and their community.

Socially responsible employee management: case studies from Saudi Arabia and Lebanon

Internal social responsibility, particularly in relation to dignified employment and the treatment of internal employees, is an important facet of CSR that has also not received the sort of dedicated attention that it rightly deserves. When it comes to CSR, attention is invariably skewed and titled toward the external activities and interventions of the firm. But how businesses deal with their internal stakeholders is as important, if not more important, given that this provides the underpinning and foundation for genuine and effective external CSR. In Chapter 5, Marian Eabrasu and Akram Al Ariss explore, through two case studies in Saudi Arabia and Lebanon, the key highlights of their employee management practices. Their findings reveal that the values of care and compassion, commonly embedded in cultural traditions, also permeate and flavor the existing employment relationships of SMEs in the region, which translates into managerial practices that revolve around trust, caring, compassion and reciprocity that are akin to internal CSR. What is interesting to note, according to the authors, is that these values are extracted from the larger culture, imported inside the organization and translated into responsible human-resource management practices, which then have a positive effect on employee commitment and enthusiasm in the workplace. The authors conclude that this kind of intuitively responsible human-resource management model is characteristic of SMEs in the region and provides a foundation for a strongly anchored internal and external CSR practice.

Corporate environmental responsibility in Jordan: the potential and the limits

With the global population rising precipitously, Earth's natural systems are increasingly depleted and in serious and accelerating decline. In the last 30 years alone, a third of the planet's natural resources – Earth's natural wealth – have been consumed. We have exceeded the sustainable yield thresholds of natural ecosystems (including water, oceans, fisheries, forests and green lands) and in the process compromised the well-being and sustainability of future generations. In Chapter 6, Muna Hindiyeh, Malyuba Abu Daabes and Haitham Salti aptly point out that the business sector is one of the biggest culprits of environmental degradation and that it needs to be a partner in sustainability going forward. The authors therefore advocate the concept of corporate environmental responsibility (CER) in the Jordanian context, and analyze CER approaches in the pharmaceutical sector through two case studies. Their findings suggest that the market drivers of CER are relatively weak in Jordan, translating into a limited awareness and understanding of the concept and its potential applications. They also emphasize that the social strand of CSR is still more appreciated and valued across the Middle East than the environmental dimension. They recommend, in conclusion, different forms of cross-sector collaboration between the public, the public sector, environmental non-governmental organizations and advocacy groups to promote the importance of CER across the Middle East.

The development of CSR reporting in the Middle East

The issue of corporate social reporting assumes a particularly important role in the context of an increasingly progressive CSR discourse.
The advancement of CSR is no doubt related to an evolution on
the corporate social reporting side, which is likely to have a positive spillover effect on perceptions of transparency, legitimacy and
accountability in the context of CSR. In Chapter 7, Jeannette Vinke
and Aida El Khatib provide an overview of CSR reporting tools globally and examine from there the current status of CSR reporting in
the Middle East. They zoom in specifically on CSR reporting practices
in the United Arab Emirates (UAE) as a case in point. Their findings
highlight that the practice of CSR reporting is still underdeveloped
in the UAE context, and that while many companies are extremely
charitable and pay various forms of *zakat* and *sadaqa*, their religious
and cultural traditions call on them to be discrete about their giving. In other words, companies across the Middle East practice what
is commonly referred to as 'silent CSR' or 'sunken CSR', as dictated
by religious practices, which is in turn impeding the maturation and
institutionalization of CSR reporting. The authors conclude by sharing the main highlights of two nascent CSR reporting initiatives from
the Middle East – the Saudi Responsible Competitiveness Index and
the Hawkamah Environmental, Social and Governance Index. They
conclude by highlighting the need for increased awareness about the
importance of CSR reporting, particularly among the home-grown
SMEs that constitute the backbone of the Middle Eastern economy.

The American University of Beirut Neighborhood
Initiative: social responsibility in a university's backyard

The ideas of giving back and good corporate citizenship certainly
have relevance and applicability to a wider spectrum of societal
actors and institutions beyond private business firms. A wide range
of actors representing different sectors and institutions are increasingly challenged to be engaged and useful in addressing relevant
and thorny societal gaps and challenges. The authors of Chapter 8,
Tonnie Choueiri and Cynthia Myntti, highlight the cross-fertilization
of ideas between the business and academic worlds, and how the
ascendancy of CSR has certainly encouraged organizations of many

types, including universities, to look within and reinvigorate their own social involvement. The authors aptly point out that by their very mission, universities advance knowledge (and societies) and therefore have a broader duty to use their resources to attend to public needs and thorny challenges in the community. An engaged and responsible university posture requires, according to the authors, several pre-requisites: collaboration to nurture problem-solving capacity; priority setting; leveraging internal faculty resources successfully; identifying problems that lie at the intersection of faculty interests and neighbors' needs; attending to power disparities; and adequate institutional support for effective engagement. The authors take the American University of Beirut Neighborhood Initiative as a case in point, explaining how it has managed, despite its young age, to successfully mobilize university resources for the public good. They also aptly capture the powerful parallels between CSR and university engagement initiatives, anchored in the common realization that the well-being and strength of an institution is intricately connected to the well-being and stability of its surrounding neighborhood.

1

CSR and Philanthropy: Different Forms of Effective Social Investment

Sari Kassis and Yazan Majaj

Introduction

Corporate social responsibility (CSR) is gaining momentum in the Middle East due to the growing global demand for sustainable human development and because societies are demanding greater accountability for the behavior of corporations. This perceptual and behavioral shift among the stakeholders reflects the increasingly sophisticated and widespread understanding of the environmental, social and labor responsibilities of corporations. This has resulted in companies being evaluated not only on the basis of their economic performance but also on the form and level of their social investment and corporate citizenship.

As practitioners in the field of CSR development, we have based our business of designing and implementing such programs and projects on the notion that CSR is a commitment to a sustainable approach that establishes holistic systems of operation for companies; it is not simply a management trend that can be adopted or abandoned at will or used strictly as a public relations gimmick. Furthermore, it is not a substitute or a more evolved version of the philanthropic traditions and customs found in the area, but rather a complementary practice that, when matched with the traditional social investment customs, results in a system tailored to address the immediate and strategic needs and challenges of local communities and resources.

11

The public good: origins and development of the local philanthropic systems

While it is difficult to identify the moment when the capitalist sector became predominant in the Arab Middle East, Arab countries started developing their economies as substantial and well-developed systems early in the 20th century. This was largely a result of the combined push by the Ottoman Empire to modernize its economy through adopting many of the European capitalist systems and structures, and the direct effect of the European colonization of the region (Rodinson, 1966, p. 159). Capitalism, in one form or another, has had a long presence in Arab societies. The predominance of the capitalism of production, when 'industrial enterprise [is] organized in accordance with the capitalist mode of production', started to take effect with the rise of state capitalism and the beginnings of industrialization in the early 19th century (Rodinson, 1966, p. 159). While the initial push toward state-owned industries was short-lived, it managed to create an impetus in which a new bourgeois class, formed in the towns from professionals such as traders and businessmen and members of the liberal professions such as lawyers and engineers, was incorporated into nationalistic economic initiatives by wealthy landowners, such as Tal'at Harb's Banque Misr in Egypt (Rodinson, 1966, p. 62).

These transformations were critiqued extensively by intellectuals of the time. Much of the literature was aimed at reconciling the advances that modern capitalism and industrialization provided with their associated 'social disintegration, acquisitiveness and class resentment . . . all seen as symptoms of a rampant materialism, intertwined with the understanding of individualism promoted by capitalism' (Tripp, 2006, p. 55). Influential writers like Rifa'a al-Tahtawi approved of the 'material progress, with developments in the productive potential of the land and the establishment of industry' as long as they were compatible with the common good (Tripp, 2006, p. 24). This essential and influential concept, while built on an idealized belief, continued to develop as it tried to reconcile the perceived benefits of capitalism with its obvious pitfalls. This led the mercantile and bourgeois classes present in the region, with their evolved businesses and industries still built around private family or individual-based ventures, to continue to satisfy their obligations toward public benefit, or public good, through the different cultural and religious mechanisms and approaches that build on Islamic tradition and its local interpretations.

Traditional mechanisms to dedicate financial and material contributions to the less privileged in societies, such as *zaqat, sadaqa, waqf* and direct charitable contributions, have all served as channels for the merchant classes and their corporations to satisfy their obligations toward society for reasons that could be social, spiritual or pragmatic (Khan, 2007). While these philanthropic tools have evolved over the years, the foundational principle – that individuals and corporations have mandated social responsibilities – has remained relatively constant. It could be argued that these norms, values and practices are contributing to facilitating the incorporation of CSR programs.

The effect of multinational corporations on CSR in the Middle East

While CSR is a relatively new concept in the Arab Middle East, multinationals operating in the region are familiar with CSR from their operations in the West (Ronnegard, 2010). While local corporations have developed a higher awareness of concepts relating to CSR, few have engaged in the field. This trend is evidenced by a 2006 study conducted by the Dubai Ethics Resource Center on CSR in the United Arab Emirates (UAE). Furthermore, it was found that while multinational corporations (MNCs) did have some local CSR programs that distinguished them from local companies, which largely engaged in corporate philanthropy, they have largely conformed to local traditional philanthropic activities (Ronnegard, 2010). However, the distinction is important and has led to the introduction of CSR as a defined and standardized concept with new sets of skills and tools that could directly benefit local philanthropic practice. As will be discussed in the case studies presented in this chapter, we believe that this introduction has been an important step toward developing philanthropy into a system of strategic giving and to consolidate it with CSR programs governed by coordinated and structured policies and institutions.

Philanthropy and CSR: partners in social investment

Can CSR and corporate philanthropy co-exist? The local companies showcased in this chapter believe that they can and that they should.

They cite the overwhelming demand for charitable and philanthropic resources in the Middle East, coupled with the region's historical affiliation with religious and cultural practices integrated within the collective social structure and dynamics, as valid reasons for the continued engagement in philanthropy and charity.

In light of the pressing social, economic, cultural and political dynamics of the Arab Middle East and the limited capacity of most governments to respond to the growing demands of their populations, we believe that pressure on the private sector to invest all kinds of resources in the full range of philanthropic and charitable choices and causes will consistently rise. This was demonstrated by the UAE government when it said that 'the private sector social duty has not yet taken roots deep enough to translate into tangible contribution to Abu Dhabi, and the UAE in general ... the social role is still absent for 99% of private firms' (Ronnegard, 2010, p12).

How this has translated on the ground is evident in the examples of two local corporations, the Nuqul Group and Abdali PSC. In both these cases, the management of the companies have clear and distinct definitions for philanthropy and CSR and recognize the value of both of these aspects of social investment. Furthermore, we have provided an example of good CSR practice, as applied by Jordan Oil Shale Company (JOSCo) – a wholly owned subsidiary of Royal Dutch Shell – and identified the elements that are informing the development.

Local corporations, corporate citizenship and CSR

Local corporations that we have worked with have reflected the wider culture dominating many corporations in the region, namely operating within and building upon the collective dynamic that exists within the Arab Middle East. These corporations reflect the dominance of the familial, tribal and group paradigms that continue to influence social status and mobility for a significant portion of the population. Consequently, local companies and their top decision makers continue to engage in philanthropic activity with great zeal. As demonstrated in the Nuqul Foundation and Abdali case studies, the adherence of decision makers within these companies to the collective ethic, and their appreciation and understanding of the local context and associated needs, reinforces the strong drive toward philanthropy and charity within local companies. These decision makers are generally involved in the collective social tradition of reinforcing social cohesion and the social structures of collective networks and dynamics. We have found that it is not uncommon to find managers at companies championing for the dedication of resources for philanthropic and charitable causes that they are affiliated with socially or culturally. This is rarely perceived negatively, especially if the cause is wide-ranging and socially acceptable.

Nonetheless, the two companies have also distinguished themselves by having an evolved and structured approach to philanthropy as well as an internal and external CSR program that adheres to international CSR standards and guidelines. Innovative environmental approaches have been deployed in all their areas of work and their employee remuneration and advancement schemes are superior to the market.

The Nuqul Group and the Elia Nuqul Foundation[1]

Background

Since the founding of his first company, which eventually grew to become the Nuqul Group, Elia Nuqul has expressed a commitment to the cause of education. For more than 50 years he has provided full and partial scholarships to students from the Nuqul family and families of company employees and to underprivileged students in Jordan, before institutionalizing his philanthropic activities in the Elia Nuqul Foundation.

The foundation, with its expressed aim to equip Jordanian youths with the skills, tools and knowledge to excel and positively impact on their socio-economic well-being, has built on the philanthropic tradition of the Nuqul Group and developed it into a systematic and strategic practice of giving (Nuqul Group, 2010). The foundation primarily covers its costs through dedicating a percentage of all family members' profits from the Nuqul Group annually; it is overseen by a board of trustees made up of four members of the Nuqul family and four volunteer experts in education and sustainable development.

Philanthropic activities

The foundation operates through two streams of interventions: the Elia Nuqul Scholarship Fund and the Social Entrepreneurship Program. The scholarship fund offers full scholarships to students from underprivileged communities, as well as providing professional training on employability and entrepreneurial skills to its network of fellows and alumni. The Social Entrepreneurship Program advocates the development of a sound social entrepreneurship sector in Jordan, and promotes social entrepreneurship by encouraging students and scholars to engage in the development of their own communities and neighborhoods.

The modality of these philanthropic programs has evolved with the experience gained. The Nuqul Group has effectively systemized its philanthropic activities and institutionalized its policy practices, culminating in the establishment of the foundation and the expansion of its mandate to introduce CSR practice to philanthropic activities and creating a joint approach between the two systems to address its area of focus. Key elements of its philanthropic activities have been systemized and combined with CSR elements to provide a comprehensive effort that directly affects the needs addressed by these programs. Some of these needs include the development of clear academic and socio-economic conditions of eligibility for students while providing them academic and psychosocial counseling. In addition, board of trustee members volunteer their time and resources to engage students in a comprehensive process that aims to ensure that students continue to meet their academic eligibility criteria while providing them with the necessary support to engage in volunteerism, social entrepreneurship and the development of their employability skills while they attend vocational or undergraduate studies. Further to this, Nuqul formed a specialized committee that manages the philanthropic process to ensure philanthropic and charitable donations are consistent and responsive to incoming requests from associations and individuals asking for aid or support.

CSR within the Nuqul Group

While institutionalizing philanthropic and charitable activities, the Nuqul Group has also adopted CSR as part of its strategic commitment to grow in a responsible and sustainable manner. In 2008, the Nuqul Group joined the UN Global Compact and has integrated its fundamental principles within its operational framework. The group annually reports on its commitments toward the compact and has systematically aligned social responsibility, employee welfare and environmental considerations within its business plans, operations and strategic directions.

The Micro-Venture Fund: from ad hoc needs to sustainable social investment.   In 2010, the Nuqul Group established the Micro-Venture Fund project as part of its ongoing commitment to CSR. This project offers capacity building platforms for entrepreneurs from Al Koura district in Jordan to transform their learning into ventures aimed at impacting on their lives positively. Some 300 projects were identified to participate in the preparation phase, which was followed by a shortlisting stage to identify 60 prospective projects for microfinancing. Nuqul Group managers and executives were invited to review and assess the prospective projects and were directly responsible for choosing the most qualified projects that met the defined criteria of social impact, innovation and commercial potential for success and growth. With 23 projects qualifying for financing, the fund was able to have a direct impact on 60 community residents with a total of 300 direct beneficiaries (Nuqul Group, 2010).

CSR and philanthropy

The Nuqul Group along with the Elia Nuqul Foundation demonstrate a clear understanding of corporate philanthropy, in both positive and negative terms, and CSR. Philanthropy, as defined by the company and in line with established social norms, is the

> effort or inclination to increase the wellbeing of humanity through charitable aid or donations. It is a short term activity that stems out of passion and commitment to help underprivileged individuals. [Although] it does not necessarily have a sustainable impact, it does generate an immediate positive effect in reaching out to communities.

Even though philanthropy is envisaged by the company as part of their overall CSR platform, it is evident that the company practically demonstrates a clear and well-differentiated understanding of philanthropy and CSR. Either through external CSR programs that involve the direct engagement of staff and management or through its Scholarship and Entrepreneurship Funds, the foundation and the Nuqul Group are clear examples of how philanthropic activities can be mainstreamed into a professional and sustainable approach that responds to the most pressing challenges of human development in the region and functions congruently with CSR programs.

Abdali PSC

Background

A more recent local player in the Jordanian market is the Abdali Investment and Development PSC. Unlike the Nuqul Group, Abdali is not a family-based corporation, yet it has reached a similar conclusion to Nuqul's management regarding its social investment strategy. Like Nuqul, Abdali considers CSR an essential business practice, and it has been incorporated into its strategic direction since the launch of the company. Abdali's CSR program was developed in line with, and in some cases has exceeded, international best practice. In addition to this, however, the company has maintained a consistent investment in philanthropic activities and continues to consider societal needs as an important and persistent driver for their continued engagement in philanthropy.

Philanthropic activities

Abdali defines philanthropy as: 'Providing support to individuals, organizations or companies operating in a not-for-profit capacity working toward improving the general well-being of a person, family, community or the larger society.'

Since its launch in 2004, Abdali has engaged in direct financial support for the King Hussein Cancer Center's youth programs and has sponsored cultural and athletic activities, including the Amman Comedy Festival and the Amman International Marathon. In addition, support was provided to establish school libraries in Jordan and to support the activities of the Arab Group for the Protection of Nature.

Like the Nuqul Group, Abdali PSC perceives corporate philanthropy as a priority concern that responds to the immediate needs of society. Mr Fahmi al-Saif, marketing manager at Abdali, explains that 'needs are heavily considered'.

Abdali and CSR: integration into all aspects of business

When it comes to CSR, Abdali defines it as 'acknowledging that a company is part of the community that they work within and that there is a natural obligation to contribute toward the betterment of its community.' CSR programs are initiated by the company and incorporated into the overall business strategy and management, and staff are actively involved in their implementation.

Abdali developed its CSR program and entered into a number of strategic partnerships, each feeding into a project relevant to both Abdali and its partner organization. Examples of this include the Alwan al Abdali project, partnerships with Relief International and Schools On-Line, Najah al Abdali and Save the Children – all projects and partnerships that use CSR tools and institutions to help deliver on the company's social obligations to its chosen focus on the region's youth and related issues.

A flagship project is the Abdali Innovation Award,[2] which was piloted in the academic year 2008–2009 as part of the CSR efforts of the company. The award aimed to stimulate innovation and creativity among Jordanian university engineering and architecture students through a competitive process that focuses on the latest and most relevant trends in architecture and engineering. The ongoing goal of the award is to develop market-relevant skills for future architects and engineers to enhance their employability and provide consultants, contractors and engineers with qualified graduates capable of undertaking challenging projects that go beyond design to efficient functionality.

Jordan Oil Shale Company

JOSCo, a wholly owned subsidiary of Royal Dutch Shell, is one of the largest MNCs working in the energy sector in the Middle East region. In 2008, Shell signed the Oil Shale Concession Agreement with the Jordanian government and registered a local subsidiary corporation tasked with implementing the agreement along with exploring the economic feasibility of their business in the area. Integral to the agreement, and one of the reasons cited for the concession offered, was an obligation for JOSCo to develop a clear, viable and effective social investment strategy for Jordan based on Shell's priority areas, namely:

- relevant capacity building;
- the natural environment; and
- road safety.

Shell is a member of the International Petroleum Industry Environmental Conservation Association (IPIECA) and has developed a global social performance policy that serves as an umbrella for all social investment programs that the corporation and its affiliates implement all over the world. While they explicitly reject corporate philanthropy as a viable social investment option, despite generating 'short-term positive local public relations...it is ineffective both in terms of gaining sustained local community support as well as leaving a long-term impact' (IPIECA, 2008, p. 11).

However, Shell recognizes the distinct benefits it can extend to regional discourse through the CSR programs of its local companies. As Tamim Suyyagh, head of corporate affairs at JOSCo, stated the benefits of 'the systematic transfer of cutting edge knowledge from a global energy company to local stakeholders [through] the advancement of relevant local capacities [by] partnering with national and local stakeholders throughout the whole process of planning, deploying and monitoring and evaluating social investment strategies and projects'. It is important to note here that what is being posited by the authors is that applying the best practices and globally tested approaches that optimize social investment strategies is not only a benefit for local CSR programs, but can also hold important ideas for the evolution of philanthropy as well.

Conclusions

What these companies and their CSR and philanthropic projects and programs serve to demonstrate is that social investment is not and should not be treated as a zero-sum game. The three companies mentioned represent three of the larger categories of businesses currently operating in the region: family owned, privately owned regional conglomerate and large MNC. On the one hand the Nuqul Group and Elia Nuqul Foundation have taken their long tradition of philanthropy and acting on a demand-based approach and developed it into an integrated institutional model that functions alongside a CSR program; Abdali PSC, on the other hand, represents a local corporation that largely adopted CSR as the main thrust of its social investment strategy but still maintains a program of corporate philanthropy. Both these groupings have also demonstrated a keen local understanding of the issues and challenges facing regional societies today.

JOSCo, though, has steered clear of philanthropic financial contributions and prefers to channel the overwhelming majority of its social investment resources into internal and external CSR programs. However, JOSCo's social investment strategy is a clear example of the value that MNCs offer to local CSR and corporate philanthropy dynamics.

The weak capacity of many governments to address the livelihood needs of all their citizens imposes added responsibilities on local businesses; and the sense of citizenship of local companies extends beyond the nominal entity of the company to a significant portion of their employees who come from the local societies and continue to engage in social dynamics throughout their employment. By applying best practices and globally tested approaches to their CSR and philanthropy efforts alike, local corporations can surely enhance and sustain the positive impact that their different social investments have on local stakeholders and local issues.

Our experience in the areas of CSR, social investment strategies and human development work has convinced us that incorporating corporate philanthropy under the large umbrella of CSR is counter-beneficial. Focusing exclusively on CSR in the Middle East undermines the deep-rooted role that philanthropists have played in the pursuit of mutual benefit and the public good. What is possibly needed is to continue to move along two tracks, preserving and leveraging existing philanthropy, and gradually directing it more effectively and strategically in serving the needs of society and the larger common good.

Recommendations

So what can the Middle East business sector learn from the CSR approaches of MNCs like JOSCo and from local, regional corporations like Abdali PSC and the Nuqul Group?

In short, there are four functionally essential elements that should be considered:

1. voluntary participation in formulating sector-wide guidelines and policies;
2. the efforts of MNCs in drafting and enforcing company specific policies, guidelines, strategies and compliance standards that their different arms, projects and assets adopt and implement;
3. the willingness of companies to transfer essential knowledge and best practice to stakeholders in and around their areas of operations; and

4. the ongoing communication and sharing of best practice within the larger network of players within and across companies working in the same sector.

These are important approaches and tools that philanthropy and CSR programs throughout the Middle East can learn from MNCs.

In the ideal scenario, corporate philanthropy should not be integrated within CSR; its historical, cultural and social implications and influences are significant enough to justify the development of a comprehensive and standardized approach and platform for action that functions hand-in-hand with CSR programs and transforms them into programs of strategic giving, so to speak.

Arab businesses that dedicate resources to philanthropic activities do so in response to the incredible demand for all kinds of resources required for social, educational, cultural, academic and emergency relief issues. Different national, regional and international reports place most of the Arab world at the bottom with regard to many vital indicators, including poverty, illiteracy and hunger.

The large socio-economic disparity in the Arab Middle East, coupled with an increasingly young and impoverished population with insufficient prospects for employment and access to livelihood resources, is not only a challenge that has to be addressed by governments and political leaders; it is an all-encompassing threat to any hope for stability and progress and all major players in various key sectors are being forced to realize that 'business as usual' is not an acceptable option. With the Arab Spring imposing unprecedented changes on political systems in the Arab Middle East, corporate philanthropy needs to be formed into a well-defined approach and coupled with CSR, as opposed to being replaced by it.

To this end, it is becoming increasingly clear to business leaders across the Middle East that corporate citizenship and social investment, be it through CSR programs or philanthropic activities, are increasingly becoming standard business practices that need to be incorporated within governance structures, planning processes and resource allocations. As local and regional companies throughout the Middle East have been gradually adopting CSR policies, it is not uncommon for these companies to confuse corporate philanthropy with aspects of CSR and opt for one over the other without having a clear understanding of the advantages or limitations of either, within the specific context of the area. It has been our experience in the field that leads us to believe that indigenous businesses should not, and generally will not, withdraw from philanthropic and charitable work. The requirement for delivering an effective CSR or philanthropic project remains the development of a deeper and clearer understanding of what both these concepts are.

The Arab private sector is in a unique position to participate in developing an all-encompassing approach to planning, channeling and monitoring philanthropic resources. Alongside the public sector, civil society and academic institutions across the Arab Middle East and North Africa, the time and circumstances are ripe, if not dangerously demanding, for these sectors to engage in serious research and development that culminates in sets of standard, credible and widely attractive approaches and methodologies to philanthropy and charity. As with the evolution of CSR, the home-grown practice of philanthropy needs in-depth research and locally responsive analysis of all historical, religious, cultural and social aspects of the practice. This will then create linkages with local and national planning processes and sustainable development plans and facilitate the development of a well-defined and effectively correlated body of knowledge on philanthropy and charity that can be reliably utilized for developing standards and approaches.

The practical applications of the approaches should ensure that philanthropic and charitable causes are aligned with local, national and regional priorities that ensure a dignified quality of life for all citizens. Philanthropic resources should be pooled in an optimal way that minimizes the duplication of efforts and the wasting of resources so that the widest possible segment of citizens can harmoniously and smoothly participate in the implementation process, whether as providers or recipients of these resources.

This effort will facilitate the development of clear definitions of updated and contemporary concepts, terms, approaches and tools that the private sector, as well as all other relevant sectors and players, can adopt and apply when engaging in philanthropic and charitable action.

Adapting the knowledge and methodologies developed through such a process into standards and best practice that are widely accepted, adopted and implemented will pave the way for formulating an accountability cycle that guarantees that high-impact targets are set and realized. It will also ensure that all actions are systematically monitored and evaluated in a manner that allows for the exponential and scientific development and growth of philanthropy into the structured, self-evolving, and needs-responsive mainstream practice that can direct and optimize the good-will potential and resources of the individual, corporate, academic, cultural, social and public-serving citizens of the Arab world. We believe that it is through this path that the most effective and clearly understood social investment programs are structured, adopted and implemented.

Notes

1. One of the co-authors of this chapter, Yazan Majaj, serves as a volunteer member of the board of trustees of the Elia Nuqul Foundation in his capacity as a development expert.
2. This was a project designed and implemented by Q perspective, the company which both authors of this chapter work for.

References

IPIECA (2008) Creating Successful, Sustainable Social Investment: Guidance Document for the Oil and Gas Industry, authored by L Zandvliet. http://commdev.org/files/2064_file_SocialInvestmentGuide.pdf, date accessed July 15, 2011.

A Khan (2007) Hill and Knowlton, http://blogarchive.hillandknowlton.com/blogs/ampersand/pages/corporate-social-responsibility-in-the-middle-east.aspx, date accessed 20 September 2011.

Nuqul Group (2010) Communication in Progress Report 2010, http://www.nuqulgroup.com/LinkClick.aspx?fileticket=PLd%2F1dWdKvY%3D&tabid=61, date accessed September 8, 2011.

M Rodinson (1966) reproduced in English (2007) as *Islam and Capitalism* (London: Saqi Books), pp. 158, 159, 162.

D Ronnegard (2010) CSR in the UAE, http://csrleaders.com/?p=259, date accessed December 7, 2011.

C Tripp (2006) *Islam and the Moral Economy* (Cambridge: Cambridge University Press), pp. 24, 55.

2
Harnessing Values for Impact Beyond Profit in MENA

David L. Haskell, Janice Hayashi Haskell
and Jessica Jinju Pottenger

Introduction

Are values such as love and respect just sentimental marketing slogans? Or is their practice pivotal to sustained impact in societies challenged by chronic unemployment, sectarian conflict, youth marginalization, gender discrimination and overburdened social services? We propose that social enterprises can have an impact on emerging markets such as the Middle East and North Africa (MENA) by the consistent practice of values. Management and economic development literature indicates that the practice of values enhances business performance. An innovative Egyptian social enterprise, Care with Love, made values central to its business model to equip undereducated and marginalized women and young people for employment as home caregivers for the housebound elderly and chronically ill. Encouraging the practice of values with a culturally rooted and spiritually inspired curriculum generated statistically significant improvements in caregiver performance. This case illustrates that values can be defined by participation, designed intentionally, contextualized inclusively and reinforced consistently, resulting in enhanced performance and mission impact. Analysis indicates that integration of values can fuel participation, invite engagement, sustain commitment, foster leadership, multiply returns and transform community. Implications are suggested for the contextualized integration of values in social enterprises in MENA.

Literature review

A growing body of research affirms that the practice of values plays a significant role in both human development and business outcomes. Terms such as 'value added' and 'value creation' are common, but the definition and role of values remains ambiguous and often controversial. At the outset, therefore, this review defines the term 'value' from the literature.

Williams, a professor of sociology at Cornell University, defines a value as 'criteria or standards of performance,' and elaborates, 'all values have cognitive, affective, and directional aspects' and 'serve as criteria for selection in action' (Williams, 1979, p. 16). Hofstede, an IBM intercultural values researcher, similarly defines values as 'feelings with an added arrow indicating a plus and a minus side' (Hofstede et al., 2010, p. 9). Grondona, a political law professor at the University of Buenos Aires, defines a value as 'an element within a conventional symbolic system that serves as a criterion for selecting among the alternatives available in a given situation' (Grondona, 2000, p. 45). In summary, values are defined as learned, interconnected, informational, affective guidelines that influence decision-making.

On a global level, values surveys indicate that a society's values influence its cultural and socio-economic development. Rokeach pioneered the exploration of values in organizations and social movements, and the role of self-awareness in values assimilation (Rokeach, 1979). Hofstede isolated cultural values in national samples from 116,000 IBM questionnaires in more than 50 countries (Hofstede, 2001; Hofstede et al., 2010). Harrison's global research argues that values shape socio-economic development (Harrison and Huntington, 2000; Harrison and Berger, 2006; Harrison and Kagan, 2006). The 2005 World Values Survey, analyzing data from more than 100 countries, indicated that cultural values, including those expressed in religious terms, significantly impact on human behavior and development (Inglehart and Welzel, 2005).

At the organizational level, management research has identified the strategic role of values in contributing to leadership quality, organizational performance and business outcomes. The GLOBE Study of more than 17,000 people in 62 countries documented the impact of values on the practice of leadership in organizations (House et al., 2004). Peters and Waterman found that 62 best-in-class US corporations were 'built around a core of "shared values"', concluding that 'excellent companies seem to have developed cultures that have incorporated the values and practices of great leaders' (Peters and Waterman, 1982, pp. 15, 26). Likewise, Collins and Porras discerned that 18 visionary 'built to last' US corporations known for outperforming their peers in shareholder returns also practiced an ideology of uncompromised values and perpetual purpose, not mere profit maximization (Collins and Porras, 1994, pp. 40–79). In a sequel study of 11 'good to great' US companies, Collins discovered that their executives practiced company core values, and prioritized values in management recruitment and discipline maintenance (Collins, 2001, pp. 193–201). Fannie Mae and Circuit City, 'good to great' companies that failed to practice their values, proved unable to sustain performance. Supplementary literature also advocates the integration of authentic values into corporate cultures and operations to improve performance (O'Toole, 1995; Blanchard and O'Connor, 2003; George, 2003; Barrett, 2006; Schein, 2010).

At the small and medium enterprise (SME) level, research also demonstrates that the practice of values has a primary influence on business outcomes. Across Latin America, nearly half of 1330 SME owner-managers in eight countries named ethical and religious values as the primary driver of their CSR practices, and indicated that these enhanced profitability, stakeholder relations and concern for employees (Vives, 2005, pp. 8–9). In Spain, four SME owners recognized for exemplary socio-environmental practices reported similar drivers, generating competitive differentiation, improved employee motivation and better economic returns (Murillo and Lozano, 2006). In the UK, 24 SME owner-managers with exemplary CSR records asserted that 'their values were essential and a powerful driver of ethics and standards in the company', resulting in improved reputation, market position, efficiency and employee motivation and recruitment (Jenkins, 2006, pp. 249–251).

Recent evidence from the MENA region also confirms the strategic role of values in business outcomes. Aramex, a CSR pioneer in Jordan, integrated values into its culture and operations by focusing less on 'share value than shared values', investing in developing its people and pursuing sustainability via interwoven stakeholder interests (Jamali and Dawkins, 2011, pp. 5–6). Likewise, six Lebanese

SME owner-managers noted for their CSR engagement reported the influence of the founder's spiritual or religious values on business performance, reinforced by relational stakeholder networks (Jamali et al., 2009). In a job satisfaction survey, 201 white-collar Egyptian workers reported humanistic and collectivist value motivations rather than monetary rewards (Sidani and Jamali, 2010).

Whether the context is global or local, Western or Eastern, corporate or SME, a recurring theme in the literature is the spiritual or religious roots of values driving socio-economic outcomes. World Values Survey researchers advise that 'the traditional secularization thesis needs updating. It is obvious that religion has not disappeared from the world, nor does it seem likely to do so' (Norris and Inglehart, 2004, p. 4). In fact, a growing body of research advocates incorporating spiritual values into organizational behavior and leadership (Kriger and Hanson, 1999; Mitroff and Denton, 1999; Neal and Biberman, 2004; Biberman and Tischler, 2008; Giacalone and Jurkiewicz, 2010). However, spiritual values integration can lead to controversy, especially in pluralist or sectarian contexts. Williams cautioned: 'We must never lose sight of the fact that values are continually used as weapons in social struggles' (Williams, 1979, p. 26). Therefore, the challenge is to sustain consensus around shared values while engaging increasingly diverse stakeholder constituencies (Haskell et al., 2009, pp. 534–538).

MENA sensitivities warrant an indigenous, contextualized business approach that integrates spiritual values while respecting diverse traditions. World Values Survey research indicates that MENA countries uphold traditional religious values and economic survival values more than any other cultural bloc (Inglehart and Welzel, 2010, p. 554). Egypt ranked first globally, with 96 per cent of Egyptians surveyed affirming the centrality of religion in their life (Handoussa, 2010, pp. 71–72). The 2010 Arab Youth Survey confirms these trends, with 82 per cent of Arab youths between the ages of 18 and 24 asserting that 'traditional values mean a lot to me, and ought to be preserved for generations to come' (ASDA'A Burson-Marsteller, 2011, p. 24). The following case study provides empirical evidence to support the literature review's conclusions, and explores how an Egyptian social enterprise incorporated a culturally rooted, spiritually inspired values assimilation process for mission impact.

Case study: Care with Love, Egypt

Vision and mission

While practicing medicine in Cairo, Dr Magda Iskander discovered the desperate need of elderly and chronically ill patients for affordable, competent and compassionate home healthcare. Iskander noticed that patients ready for hospital discharge were not being taken home because their families were unable to care for them unassisted. Several demographic trends had contributed to this. Between 1976 and 2007, life expectancy in Egypt jumped from age 55 to 71.7 (Handoussa, 2010, p. 257). Between 1988 and 2008, those in Egypt over the age of 65 increased from 3.8 to 4.1 per cent of the population (El-Zanaty and Way, 2009, p. 15). However, between 2002 and 2008, expenditure on healthcare declined from 5.99 to 4.75 per cent of gross domestic product (Ministry of Health Egypt, 2010, p. 16). The numbers and needs of the elderly and chronically ill had increased while the spending on healthcare decreased, with nothing to bridge the growing gap.

At the same time, Iskander observed the dehumanizing weight of unemployment, especially on women and youths. A 2007 survey illustrated Egypt's unemployment crisis: 62.4 per cent over those over the age of 15, with secondary education, were unemployed; 32.8 per cent with university education were unemployed; and women were twice as likely to suffer unemployment (Handoussa, 2010, p. 268). Iskander put these trends together and recognized a sustainable market-driven opportunity to create dignified employment while simultaneously meeting a pressing public health need.

Founded in 1996, Care with Love was her entrepreneurial solution. Conceived as a social enterprise, Care with Love operated under a partner non-governmental organization (NGO) until it received its own NGO registration with the Ministry of Social Affairs in 2003. Care with Love had four aims:

(a) create dignified employment for the marginalized unemployed;
(b) provide loving, competent and affordable home healthcare to house-bound clients;
(c) achieve financial sustainability from earned revenues alone; and
(d) establish home and hospice healthcare as a respected profession in Egypt.

Growth and impact

From 1996 to 2010, Care with Love made laudable progress. First, Care with Love graduated 924 caregivers in 14 years, with 691 employed directly and another 233 employed elsewhere. The marginalized benefited most from these opportunities – of those employed by Care with Love, 85 per cent lacked a secondary diploma, 83 per cent were women and nearly 43 per cent were youths aged between 17 and 25. Second, during those years, Care with Love served 1450 home healthcare clients, with demand generated entirely from satisfied referrals (Figure 2.1).

Third, although initially capitalized by start-up grants and loans, since 2006 Care with Love has achieved financial sustainability from earned revenues alone, registering double-digit earned revenue growth for each year (Figure 2.2). Fourth, the Egyptian home healthcare profession was officially recognized in 2004 when the Egyptian Ministry of Labor granted social insurance benefits to caregivers. Care with Love was also recognized internationally by Ashoka, Acumen Fund and the Ford and Sawiris Foundations in 2003; Dreams InDeed in 2007; the Arab League Summit in 2009; the US Presidential Entrepreneurship Summit in 2010; and the Clinton Global Initiative in 2011. Well on its way to achieving each of its start-up goals, Care with Love was ready to expand.

The values assimilation process

To ensure Care with Love achieved its mission, Iskander implemented intensive training for caregivers, most of whom were undereducated and marginalized women and young people. After screening for their

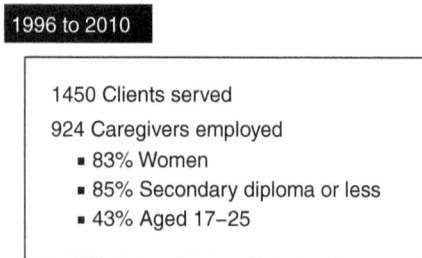

```
┌─ 1996 to 2010 ─┐
└────────────────┘

┌──────────────────────────────────┐
│ 1450 Clients served              │
│ 924 Caregivers employed          │
│    ▪ 83% Women                   │
│    ▪ 85% Secondary diploma or less│
│    ▪ 43% Aged 17–25              │
└──────────────────────────────────┘
```

Figure 2.1   The Social Impact of Care with Love

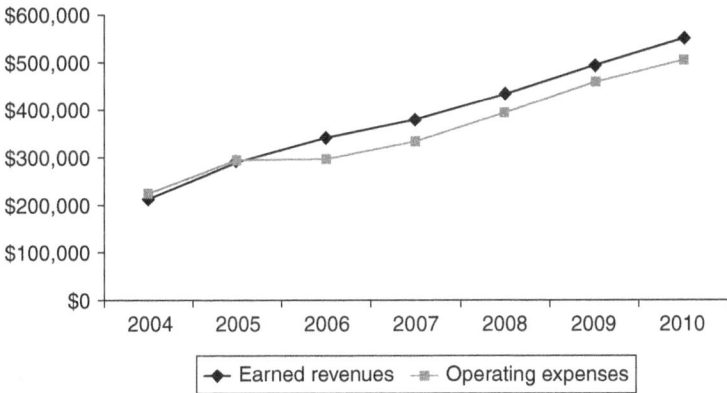

Figure 2.2 The Sustainable Profitability of Care with Love

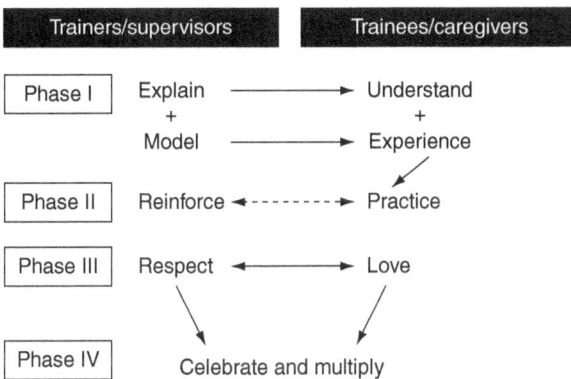

Figure 2.3 The Care with Love Values Assimilation Process

Care with Love relational aptitude, applicants entered a three-month training program on interpersonal and technical skills, including practical fieldwork and a residential retreat. Trainers included brief, ad hoc 'values reflections' at their discretion. This values assimilation process is depicted in Figure 2.3.

During Phase I, trainees were introduced to the importance of values-based behavior in their work. For some, the mere act of learning about values in behavior was profound. One caregiver reported that the training inculcated new habits of polite speech, hygienic care and responsibility for her workplace and living area. In her own words, values reflections helped her 'to become civilized'. Trainees confirmed, however, that understanding alone was insufficient; seeing the values modeled was essential. One remembered, 'We learned love by example. A caregiver had broken her hand during training; the trainer took her to the doctor and stayed until she was OK.'

Phase II provided trainees a closely supervised opportunity to practice the values and skills they had observed. This critical phase determined which caregivers would go on to work with clients, as living demonstrations of the Care with Love values and mission. Values-aligned behavior and technical skills were systematically reinforced by supervisory support, impromptu client home visits, and quarterly refresher courses. Trainer supervisors transitioned from initiating to supporting values assimilation. Supervisory support and affirmation helped caregivers sustain values alignment and take professional pride in their work. One reported: 'I was with a family and left them because of ill treatment. I did not complain nor ask for anything, but my supervisors did not let it pass and stood by me and made sure I was redressed. They support us in difficult situations.' This phase consolidated mutual benefits, with Care with Love maintaining its reputation and clientele and the caregiver receiving moral and financial support.

In Phase III, caregivers moved beyond training to fieldwork, with the motivation to continue to practice love by receiving the respect of their clients and supervisors. This exchange of love and respect transcended sectarian lines:

> When I first went to my elderly client, she refused to shake hands or relate to me because I was wearing a full veil. It shocked her, so I decided to be patient. If she refused me that was her right, but that I had to try. I removed my veil when I was with her. I was cheerful with her; slowly she accepted me. Now I go with her to church and shopping, and she even trusts me with her purse.

In Phase IV of the values assimilation process, caregivers multiplied the mission impact as they generalized the values to their personal lives outside of work: 'I began to apply these values after my work with Care with Love, such as commitment and being on time.' Because values-aligned caregivers are the heart of their mission, Care with Love also sponsored an annual community festival where caregivers and their families celebrated trainee graduations and honored outstanding caregivers. The outcome was a successful social enterprise and a burgeoning new profession.

Reinforcing core values

Most of the Cairo team leaders had been with Iskander since she founded Care with Love in 1996, and internalized the values day-by-day as they worked with her. Although they implemented the values assimilation process procedurally, specific values were not codified and presented systematically. Values reflections consisted of a notebook full of clippings, ideas and experiences gleaned over the years by Iskander and her trainers. Then, when Care with Love experimented with expansion in 2007 by franchising in another city, the quality of the care delivery suffered. Technical skills transferred readily, but the hallmark loving relationships were weak. Iskander reflected again how she had learned to demonstrate love without discrimination by religion, ethnicity, gender, age, class and disability, just as had been modeled by Jesus, her own spiritual inspiration. Iskander considered how she had been present to ensure that her Cairo team and caregivers modeled the standard for which she named the organization, *care with love*. In consultation with Dreams InDeed, Iskander concluded that the bottleneck was the current ad hoc approach that relied solely upon direct, sustained engagement with her and her team. If their services were to scale, the definition and practice of its values needed more clarity, structure and reinforcement.

Therefore, in 2007, Dreams InDeed customized and facilitated a participatory rapid appraisal (Theis and Grady, 1991) to assist Care with Love in identifying and defining its values. For the first time, their shared values were brainstormed and agreed by consensus, ranked in priority, defined in words and illustrated by exemplary behavior celebrated in their history. The outcome was clarity and unity among trainers, supervisors, staff and the board on the values that they had been practicing but which until then had not clearly codified. The resulting six Care with Love core values included:

- **Faithfulness, integrity in word and deed** is vital to earn trust when taken into a family home, such as when a caregiver found and returned a lost gold bracelet to a client who had forgotten about it.

- **Humility, equal respect for all** focuses on service not status, such as during the residential training retreat, when the managing director played with us with all humility, not acting as if she was a manager at all.
- **Commitment, honoring rights in word and deed** is essential to sustain endurance, such as when a caregiver persevered in serving an Alzheimer's patient for an entire year until her death, winning over her son's bad temper because she had the right to live and receive care.
- **Teamwork, collaboration for one goal** is required to achieve synergy across roles, as a caregiver expressed, 'They protect women, follow up on them, and take necessary measures with bad clients; this gave me the confidence to continue this work with patience.'
- **Acceptance of the Other, engagement with all our differences** is critical to ensure unity in diversity, such as when a caregiver noted, 'Three of four families I have served are Copts; if I had not learned to accept the Other, I would not have continued in these homes.'
- **Sacrificial love, giving without limit or condition** is 'the golden clasp that holds the string of all the other values together,' such as when 'a caregiver saw an elderly patient's health deteriorate rapidly, but had no car to take him to hospital. He ran into the streets to find an ambulance, and then remained with his patient for three days straight.'

All agreed that the development of a structured values curriculum was needed. A formalized values curriculum was a novel concept and required months of discussion, piloting and revision, including a review of cultural appropriateness by religious and educational advisors. The content for this was researched from indigenous cultural sources, including the Bible, Islamic texts, Egyptian folklore and organizational history. An Egyptian educational consultant compiled 60 values topics in four sequential sections on understanding, exploring, applying and sustaining values (El-Rifai, 2010). Values pedagogy included illustrative stories, personal reflection and non-directive group discussion to raise the awareness of values and deepen the understanding of their application.

Quantitative research

To ensure the quality of the caregiver service remotely from Cairo, Care with Love deployed a rigorous performance review system that ensured that supervisors call clients weekly, visit client homes quarterly, maintain caregiver telephone contact, require quarterly refresher courses and conduct quarterly performance evaluations. Quarterly performance was rated on a five-rank scale: excellent, very good, good, acceptable and on-list (unrated, if absent).

To assess the impact of the new values curriculum (VC) after 18 months of use, Dreams InDeed assembled researchers from Egypt, Jordan, Lebanon and the US.[1] The research hypothesis was that VC training positively correlated with improved caregiver performance. Four tests were conducted to assess the strength of the relationship between these two variables.[2] The first test measured the effect of VC training on overall caregiver performance, and found that VC training had a statistically significant influence on improved average performance (Figure 2.4).

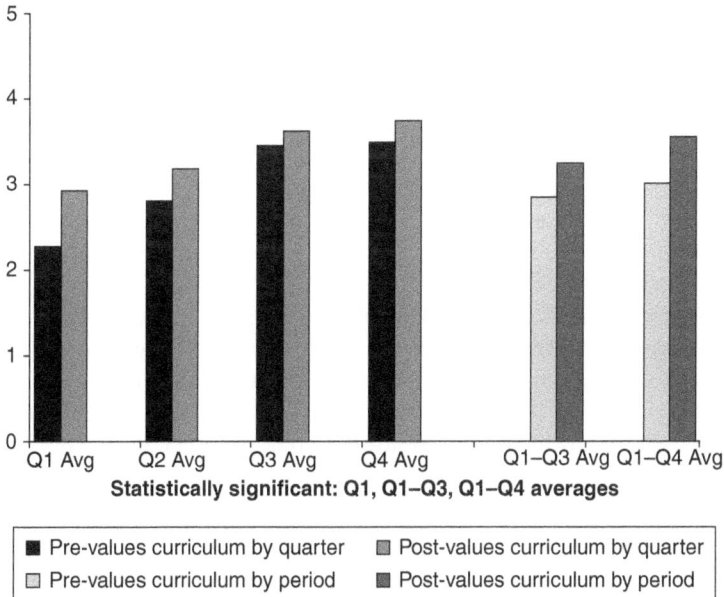

Figure 2.4 Improvement of Average Caregiver Performance

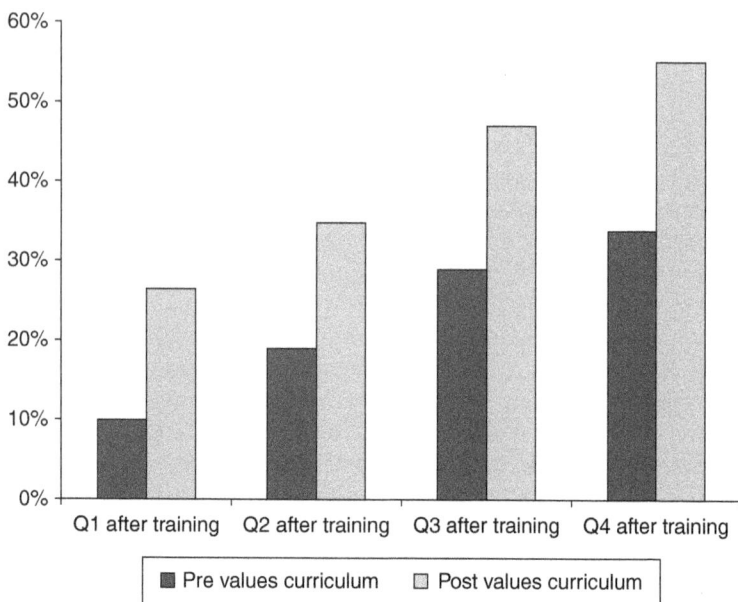

Figure 2.5   Acceleration of Excellent Caregiver Performance

The second test measured the impact of VC training on top caregiver performers, finding that VC training was particularly effective at increasing the number of caregivers performing excellently (Figure 2.5). These results indicate that VC training may accelerate performance improvements, possibly due to a more rapid building of caregiver–client trust.

The third test studied the effect of VC training on caregiver bonuses awarded, and found that the post-VC group did not receive higher bonuses after completing the training. In fact, the pre-VC group's bonuses the first year after training were larger and inconsistent with performance ratings, indicating that caregiver motivation is unrelated to monetary incentives.

Finally, tests of correlation between caregiver performance and the control variables of caregiver gender, age and education level identified no statistically significant relationships. While there might have been performance gaps on other measures, both genders and all ages and educational levels competently demonstrated Care with Love values and skills. Beyond the physical strength to lift a patient and the mental capacity to learn, the critical qualifier for Care with Love employment appeared to be values alignment, a choice available to all. With fortunate irony, those most marginalized from employment prospects – the undereducated, women and youths – often became the star caregivers.

Qualitative research

Questionnaires were also administered to caregivers, who had to rank ten factors by their influence on work performance on a five-point scale, ranging from 1 as 'none' to 5 as 'very strong'. In addition, extensive qualitative interviews were held with a full range of Care with Love stakeholders.[3] Due to the qualitative nature of the data gathered and the small sample size, statistical analysis was not appropriate, but the results clearly indicated caregiver motivation trends (Figure 2.6).

Post-VC caregivers ranked technical factors (in medium gray) as less influential on their performance than all relational factors (in light gray) and values reflections themselves (in white). Relational engagement surfaced as a primary motivator for post-VC caregivers, replacing the technical training and support as the primary motivators for

Pre-values curriculum

Rank	Factor	%
1	Skills training	98
2	Client respect	96
3	Management recognition	94
4	Supervisor evaluation	90
5	CWL uniform	90
6	Supervisor home visit	90
7	Value reflections	80
8	Role models	73
9	Compensation	71
10	Prizes	71

Post-values curriculum

Rank	Factor	%
1	Management recognition	100
2	Client respect	95
3	Supervisor evaluation	95
4	Value reflections	90
5	Skills training	90
6	Role models	85
7	CWL uniform	80
8	Supervisor home visit	75
9	Compensation	75
10	Prizes	65

Figure 2.6 Self-Reported Caregiver Motivation Rankings

pre-VC caregivers. VC training may have helped improve caregiver performance because it clarified and explained values modeled by respected supervisors, affirmed with peers and publicly honored at annual festivals. Compensation and prizes (in dark gray) were ranked least influential by both pre-VC and post-VC groups, indicating that monetary incentives are not a significant motivator of caregiver performance. As one caregiver said: 'Being happy and satisfied in a place where I find respect and human treatment is more important than money.'

In summary, the research findings suggest that a culturally rooted and spiritually inspired values curriculum, integrated as part of a holistic training process, is more likely to initiate and sustain a better performance from all trainees, and to accelerate the development of top-performers. The effect of formal values training on performance is unrelated to monetary incentives and is irrespective of the caregiver's age, gender and education level.

Analysis and implications

Empirical and interview findings are consistent with the literature indicating that the practice of values plays a significant role in both human development and business performance. We now analyze these findings to explore reasons for the relationship between the practice of values and enhanced performance, and to suggest the implications for the application of values in the emerging markets of MENA.

Aligned participation

Voluntary participation based on mutual respect helps transform business relationships from services 'bought' by compensation, to performance motivated from the heart. One veteran caregiver stressed: 'The values we have acquired are not "outside us" for work alone, but "inside us", practiced in our lives both on the job and outside work.' The values implicit in participatory processes foster a spirit of ownership, inspiring volitional alignment rather than compliance with external controls. With the advent of the information age, and now in the wake of the 2011 Arab Spring, centralized management control paradigms are proving increasingly ineffective and obsolete. Social enterprise leaders in the MENA region would do well to add participatory facilitation to their skill repertoire to discover, agree and collaborate around shared values. The effectiveness of participatory approaches is confirmed not only in this Care with Love social enterprise case, but also in many diverse international development contexts (Duraiappah et al., 2005). The key is to ensure that all stakeholders are included in the process; not only investors and directors, but also employees, clients, the public – and especially the often unheard but not insignificant voices of the marginalized. Inviting participation need not unleash disorder. The spirit of partic-ipation is deeply rooted in the Arab tradition of mutual aid (*aouneh*), when neighbors volunteer to build houses or harvest fields together. MENA social enterprises, as modeled by Care with Love, can har-ness and reactivate this tradition of cooperation for the common good. Participatory collaboration offers a viable option to balance and complement competitive approaches. As the Arab proverbs say, 'One hand cannot clap' (Bestourous, 2005, p. 81), and 'The hand of God is with the group' (Madanat, 2011).

Diversity dialog

The cultural and ethnic diversity within MENA is one of its greatest treasures and yet at the same time one of its greatest dilemmas. Wise social enterprise leaders in MENA will mine the treasure while disarm-ing the dilemma, avoiding the extremes of tyranny and anarchy as they walk the tightrope toward unity in diversity. Rather than ignor-ing inevitable controversy as taboo, social enterprise practitioners can explore centuries of experience together in the diverse traditions in MENA to search for shared values across all spectra. Culturally rooted and spiritually inspired values can encourage *all* stakeholders to engage while they also call upon *all* to change. A caregiver reported: 'While working with a Christian client, I listened with her to her Christian tapes and TV programs, and in return, she played the Islamic call to prayer on TV for me. This reinforced our mutual trust and communication and her family still contacts and asks about me.' The caregiver and her client were altered by the discovery of their shared value of respect, enabling them to differ on other principles and yet still be unified in a relationship. An Egyptian proverb aptly advises, 'He grasps the stick in the middle' (Bestourous, 2005, p. 97). That wise middle ground at Care with Love is where shared val-ues are forged in the cauldron of honest dialog about differences in sustained relationships. If and when that trust is broken, archetypical Arab hospitality and generosity affirm that the treasure of unity in diversity still warrants the painful, uphill journey back: 'If your enemy comes to your door, say "Welcome!"' (Bestourous, 2005, p. 117), and 'Reconciliation is the master of judgments' (Madanat, 2011).

Coherent policy

Values must be built in, not tacked on. Care with Love values are not brochure slogans, but essential behaviors that its people practice, its policies require and its systems support. Both supervisors and caregivers alike know that they are expected to live by the values, even if on occasion that results in lost clients, lost revenues and lost opportunities. As one caregiver reported: 'A family and client were very rude with me; I had decided to quit if my supervisors did not act justly. They investigated and then stood by me, so I realized that influence and power do not control Care with Love decisions.' This is particularly relevant in MENA, where extended family owned and operated SMEs are common. The influence of the founder's values and example can become diffused when the enterprise expands beyond the founder's relational network, as discovered during Care with Love franchising. To maintain the potency of values and sustain growth, we advise MENA social-enterprise leaders to codify and integrate their core values through coherent operating policy and systems organization-wide, defining for all the latitude of acceptable means in pursuit of the mission. Infusing values into policy and systems will leverage their impact; however, this does not replace the imperative of the living example of founders and directors. Values are better not proclaimed if they are not applied equitably for all, regardless of blood or friendship connections. The hypocritical application of values, as noted in the Egyptian folk saying, is 'Water under straw' (Bestourous, 2005, p. 271).

Adaptive leadership

The Care with Love values assimilation process helped create an environment in the MENA region where adaptive leadership emerged and developed. In spite of the stigma of manual labor in MENA, it is worth noting that all Care with Love trainers and supervisors, including the founder herself, got their hands dirty in service to the elderly and chronically ill. Caregivers internalized the values they had heard articulated and seen modeled, and took the initiative to put them into practice in new contexts, both on and off the job, monitored or solo. Values internalization equips and ensures that people can innovate to serve the mission in the face of complexity, rather than waiting for orders as compliant followers. The outcome is that the whole person engages to serve with heart and mind, not merely hands. One trainer recounted:

> Fire broke out in a building where a caregiver was at work with an elderly, disabled, sick grandmother. Her grandchildren deserted her and fled, screaming for the caregiver to save herself for the sake of her own children. However, at the risk of her life, the caregiver wrapped her patient in a blanket and carried her down the stairs, shouting, 'She's like my family; I have to save her!'

It is through values internalization that adaptive leaders multiply and take action to serve the common good, translating poetic visions of dignity into tangible results on the ground: 'Yesterday we obeyed kings and bent our necks before emperors. But today we kneel only to truth, follow only beauty, and obey only love' (Gibran and Cole, 1997, p. 30).

Shared benefit

Business has tremendous potential to serve the common good with the sustainable production of goods and services. In fact, each year since 2006, Care with Love has averaged more than half a million patient-care hours annually. They served, employed and graduated a yearly average of 137 clients, 162 caregivers and 60 new trainees, respectively. Mere statistics, however, do not express the social impact that the Care with Love practice of values has had on stakeholders. One caregiver reported:

> During practical training in a disadvantaged home, an elderly woman was dying while nurses were ignoring her. Our trainer and we trainees, who until then had feared touching anyone dying, insisted on bathing her. Her face relaxed; tears rolled down her cheeks. Stunned, we realized what our attention and care meant for her.

While Care with Love is financially profitable, its social impact in human terms arguably multiplies even more significant returns: improved health, respected elders, sustained families, effective education, dignified employment, inter-sectarian understanding, reduced government dependency and increased equity by gender, class and age. To understand the value of such social impact, a change of paradigm from myopic fixation on profit maximization to a holistic vision of shared benefit for all stakeholders is required. The beauty and complexity of shared benefit cannot be reduced to the single bottom line of profit, nor even captured in triple economic–social–environmental bottom lines. To be effective and sustainable, stakeholder value analysis and business design must be inclusive, integrated and holistic. The Care with Love values-driven model confirms the feasibility of generating not only economic profits but also diverse stakeholder benefits in the MENA region. The Arab Youth Survey lists healthcare and jobs as only two emerging markets; others cry out for enterprise innovations offering security, safety, family, marriage, housing, education, credit, jobs, gender rights, Internet, travel and more (ASDA'A Burson-Marsteller, 2011). We encourage MENA practitioners to pursue not only financial returns, but also other dimensions of market demand and mission impact, including, but not limited to, social, environmental, aesthetic, spiritual and cultural factors. Avoiding reductionist materialism, we heed the wisdom that 'the most pitiful among men is he who turns his dreams into silver and gold' (Gibran, 2010, p. 21).

Sustained trust

Care with Love values respect all people as responsible agents who participate in the creation of both economic value and social capital, the cohesion of trust which is the true wealth of any community (Fukuyama, 1995). People are not objects to be exploited for economic-value extraction. Through this lens, Iskander perceived the dignity and worth of both the chronically ill and the chronically unemployed, and their potential to create value together by serving each other. The chronically ill need and can afford to pay for some health services, but really desire loving care. The chronically unemployed need and can afford to learn some technical skills and earn a livable wage, but they really desire dignity and respect. Trading technical skills for modest wages creates some value, but the primary value creation is in the relational exchange of caregiver

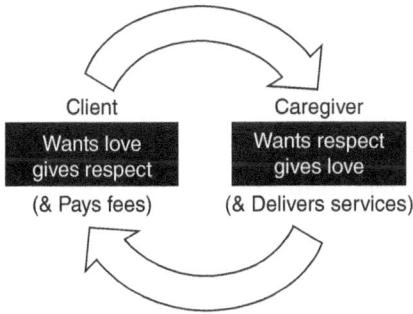

Figure 2.7 Value Exchange of Respect and Love

love and client respect in a sustained way (Figure 2.7). Values-driven development is sustainable because love and respect are both blind – unconditional and non-discriminatory.

Conclusion

Trust is the soil in which such development grows. Without trust, business is a burden and finance flees. As Gibran perceived: 'Work is love made visible. If you cannot work with love but only with distaste, it is better that you should leave your work and sit at the gate of the temple and take alms of those who work with joy' (Gibran, 1996, p. 14). The Arab Spring was an unmistakable call for well-placed trust in the MENA region. Social enterprise innovators can lead the way forward by defining complementary needs, negotiating shared benefits, forging shared values and nurturing trust back to life in pursuit of a shared vision of community, one in which there is an active exchange of higher-valued relational intangibles such as love and respect.

Acknowledgments

The authors are grateful to the following people: the generous expertise of Care with Love founder Magda Iskander and her board, trainers, supervisors, staff, caregivers and clients; Amr Hamouda, Nadia Rifaat and George Nabil of Al-Fustat Center for Studies and Consultation; Joy Hazucha of PDI Ninth House; Dima Jamali of American University of Beirut; Sarah von Hefelstein of Braver Valuation Services; Stephanie Bassil of Vanderbilt University; David

Fernandez of Princeton University; Safa Halaseh, participatory development specialist; and Yasmine El-Rifai, pedagogy specialist. This research would not have been possible without their input, but the responsibility for any errors remains ours alone.

Appendix – Research methodology

Hypothesis: **The introduction of a formal, structured values curriculum (VC) positively correlates with improved employee performance, as measured by (a) employee performance ratings and (b) employee bonuses received.** As noted in the text, caregiver performance is rated quarterly on a five-rank scale. Bonus eligibility is based on refresher-course results. Quarterly performance rating and bonus data were available from Q2 2006 to Q1 2011. For optimal comparability, data were chosen for the first four quarters after each caregiver's training, resulting in cohorts of 121 pre-VC and 49 post-VC caregivers. Four tests were run on the data gathered from these sample populations.

> *Test One*: To test the effect of VC training on overall caregiver performance, ratings were converted to 0 (absent), 1 (on list, unrated), 2 (acceptable), 3 (good), 4 (very good) and 5 (excellent). Quarterly ratings and average ratings across quarters 1–3 and quarters 1–4 were computed, and an independent samples *t*-test was then conducted. *Results*: The average quarterly performance scores of the post-VC caregiver cohort exceeded the pre-VC cohort by statistically significant margins [Q1, $t(78) = -2.29$, $p < 0.05$; mean of Q1–Q3, $t(168) = -1.98$, $p < 0.05$; and mean of Q1–Q4, $t(159) = -2.65$, $p < 0.01$]. The lack of statistical significance for quarters 2–4 can be explained due to small sample sizes spread over multiple categories. These results indicate that VC training contributed to improved average overall performance (see Figure 2.4 in the chapter).
>
> *Test Two*: To test the effect of VC training on top caregiver performers, performance ratings for pre- and post-VC cohorts were cross-tabulated for each of the first four quarters of the VC program, and a chi-square test was performed. *Results*: More of the post-VC cohort was rated excellent in each of the four quarters after training. Cross-tabulations for pre-VC and post-VC cohorts rated

excellent generated statistically significant chi-squares for the first quarter after training [$\chi^2(4, N = 170) = 10.23$, $p < 0.05$]; and the third quarter after training [$\chi^2(5, N = 170) = 11.51$, $p < 0.05$)], but not for the second and fourth quarters, again likely to the small sample sizes spread across multiple categories. As Test One showed, the improvement effect for excellent performers was clearest in the first quarter. This suggests that VC training may be linked to a faster performance ramp-up of caregivers already performing excellently (see Figure 2.5 in the chapter).

Test Three: To test the effect of VC training on caregiver bonuses awarded, an independent samples t-test was conducted. *Results*: The hypothesis that the post-VC group would receive higher bonuses after training completion was not supported, indicating that monetary incentives did not significantly influence caregiver performance.

Test Four: To test relationships between caregiver performance and control variables of caregiver gender, age and educational level, Pearson correlations were performed. *Results*: Tests indicated no statistically significant correlation between caregiver performance and the control variables of caregiver gender, age and education level.

Notes

1. Team expertise included international development, social entrepreneurship, participatory appraisal, public policy, developmental economics, organizational development, business valuation, impact investment and statistical analysis.
2. Using PDI Ninth House software, the methodology, data collection and statistical analysis were supervised by Joy Hazucha PhD, the senior vice-president for leadership research. The quantitative research methodology is recorded in the appendix.
3. Interviews were conducted and questionnaires were administered by Al-Fustat Center for Studies and Consultation to a sample of 49 pre-VC caregivers and 20 post-VC caregivers.

References

ASDA'A Burson-Marsteller (2011). *White Paper on the Third Annual Arab Youth Survey 2010*, http://www.arabyouthsurvey.com/english/ (accessed 7 May 2012).

Barrett, R. (2006). *Building a Values-Driven Organization: A Whole System Approach to Transformation* (Burlington, MA: Elsevier Butterworth-Heinemann).

Bestourous, H. (2005). *The People's Proverbs of Egypt* (Enumclaw, WA: Pleasant Word).

Biberman, J. & Tischler, L. (eds) (2008). *Spirituality in Business: Theory, Practice, and Future Directions* (New York: Palgrave Macmillan).

Blanchard, K. & O'Connor, M. (2003). *Managing by Values: How to Put Your Values into Action for Extraordinary Results, Second Edition* (San Francisco, CA: Berrett-Koehler).

Collins, J.C. (2001). *Good to Great: Why Some Companies Make the Leap . . . and Others Don't* (New York: HarperBusiness).

Collins, J.C. & Porras, J.I. (1994). *Built to Last: Successful Habits of Visionary Companies* (New York: HarperBusiness).

Duraiappah, A.K., Roddy, P.V., & Parry, J. (2005). *Have Participatory Approaches Increased Capabilities?* (Winnipeg: International Institute for Sustainable Development), http://www.iisd.org/pdf/2005/economics_participatory_approaches.pdf.

El-Rifai, Y. (2010). *Values and Principles: Between Theory and Practice* (Cairo, Egypt: Care with Love).

El-Zanaty, F. & Way, A. (2009). *Egypt Demographic and Health Survey 2008* (Cairo, Egypt: Ministry of Health, El-Zanaty & Associates, and Macro International).

Fukuyama, F. (1995). *Trust: The Social Virtues and the Creation of Prosperity* (New York: Free Press).

George, B. (2003). *Authentic Leadership: Rediscovering the Secrets to Creating Lasting Value* (San Francisco, CA: Jossey-Bass).

Giacalone, R.A., & Jurkiewicz, C.L. (2010). *Handbook of Workplace Spirituality and Organizational Performance, Second Edition* (Armonk, NY: ME Sharpe).

Gibran, K. (1996). *The Prophet* (Hertfordshire, UK: Woodsworth Editions).

Gibran, K. (2010). *Sand and Foam: and Other Poems* (Oxford: Benediction Classics).

Gibran, K. & Cole, J.R.I. (1997). *The Vision: Reflections on the Way of the Soul* (London: Arkana Penguin).

Grondona, M. (2000). 'A Cultural Typology of Economic Development', in Harrison, L.E. & Huntington, S.P. (eds), *Culture Matters: How Values Shape Human Progress* (New York: Basic Books).

Handoussa, H. (ed.) (2010). *Egypt Human Development Report 2010* (United Nations Development Programme and the Institute of National Planning Egypt), http://www.undp.org.eg/Portals/0/EHDR%202010/NHDR%202010%20english.pdf.

Harrison, L.E. & Berger, P.L. (eds) (2006). *Developing Cultures: Case Studies* (New York: Routledge).

Harrison, L.E. & Huntington, S.P. (eds) (2000). *Culture Matters: How Values Shape Human Progress* (New York: Basic Books).

Harrison, L.E. & Kagan, J. (eds) (2006). *Developing Cultures: Essays on Cultural Change* (New York: Routledge).

Haskell, D.L., Haskell, J.H., & Kwong, J.W. (2009). 'Spiritual Resources for Change in Hard Places: A Values-Driven Social Entrepreneurship Theory of Change', in Goldstein, J.A., Hazy, J.K., & Silberstang, J. (eds), *Complexity Science and Social Entrepreneurship: Adding Social Value Through Systems Thinking* (Litchfield Park, AZ: ISCE Publishing).

Hofstede, G. (2001). *Culture's Consequences: Comparing Values, Behaviors, Institutions, and Organizations Across Nations, Second Edition* (Thousand Oaks, CA: Sage Publications).

Hofstede, G., Hofstede, G.J., & Minkov, M. (2010). *Cultures and Organizations: Software of the Mind, Intercultural Cooperation and Its Importance for Survival, Third Edition* (New York: McGraw-Hill).

House, R.J., Hanges, P.J., Javidan, M., Dorfman, P.W., & Gupta, V. (2004). *Culture, Leadership, and Organization: The GLOBE Study of 62 Societies* (Thousand Oaks, CA: Sage Publications).

Inglehart, R. & Welzel, C. (2005). *Modernization, Culture Change, and Democracy: The Human Development Sequence* (New York: Cambridge University Press).

Inglehart, R. & Welzel, C. (2010). 'Changing Mass Priorities: The Link Between Modernization and Democracy', *Perspectives on Politics*, 8, 551–567.

Jamali, D. & Dawkins, C. (2011). *Sustainability in the Arab World: the ARAMEX Way*, Case 9B11M060, Richard Ivey School of Business Foundation, University of Western Ontario, London, ON, Canada.

Jamali, D., Zanhour, M., & Keshishian, T. (2009). 'Peculiar Strengths and Relational Attributes of SMEs in the Context of CSR', *Journal of Business Ethics*, 87, 355–377.

Jenkins, H. (2006). 'Small Business Champions for Corporate Social Responsibility', *Journal of Business Ethics*, 67, 241–256.

Kriger, M.P. & Hanson, B.J. (1999). 'A Value-Based Paradigm for Creating Truly Healthy Organizations', *Journal of Organizational Change Management*, 12, 302–317.

Madanat, N. (2011). UNFPA Country Support Team Advisor for the Arab States, personal interview 17 December 2011.

Ministry of Health Egypt and Health Systems 20/20. (2010). *National Health Accounts 2007/2008: Egypt* (Bethesda, MD: ABT Associates Inc.), http://www.healthsystems2020.org/content/resource/detail/2730/.

Mitroff, I. & Denton, E.A. (1999). *A Spiritual Audit of Corporate America: A Hard Look at Spirituality, Religion, and Values in the Workplace* (San Francisco, CA: Jossey-Bass).

Murillo, D. & Lozano, J. (2006). 'SMEs and CSR: An Approach to CSR in Their Own Words', *Journal of Business Ethics*, 67, 227–240.

Neal, J. & Biberman, J. (2004). 'Research that Matters: Helping Organizations Integrate Spiritual Values and Practices', *Journal of Organizational Change Management*, 17, 7–10.

Norris, P. & Inglehart, R. (2004). *Secular and Sacred: Religion and Politics Worldwide* (New York: Cambridge University Press).

O'Toole, J. (1995). *Leading Change: The Argument for Values-Based Leadership* (New York: Ballantine Books).

Peters, T.J. & Waterman, R.H. Jr. (1982). *In Search of Excellence: Lessons from America's Best-Run Companies* (New York: Harper & Row).

Rokeach, M. (1979). *Understanding Human Values: Individual and Societal* (New York: Free Press).

Schein, E.H. (2010). *Organizational Culture and Leadership, Fourth Edition* (San Francisco, CA: Jossey-Bass).

Sidani, Y.M. & Jamali, D. (2010). 'The Egyptian Worker: Work Beliefs and Attitudes', *Journal of Business Ethics*, 92, 443–450.

Theis, J. & Grady, H. (1991). *Participatory Rapid Appraisal for Community Development: A Training Manual Based on Experiences in the Middle East and North Africa* (International Institute for Environment and Development), http://pubs.iied.org/pdfs/8282IIED.pdf.

Vives, A. (2005). 'Social and Environmental Responsibility in Small and Medium Enterprises in Latin America', *The Journal of Corporate Citizenship*, 21, 39–50.

Williams, R.M. (1979). 'Change and Stability in Values and Value Systems: A Sociological Perspective', in Rokeach, M. (ed.), *Understanding Human Values: Individual and Societal* (New York: Free Press).

3
CSR to Increase Access to Medicines: Lessons and Opportunities for the Middle East

Joseph Antoun

Introduction

Corporate social responsibility (CSR) aimed at increasing access to medicines (ATM) has recently witnessed evolutionary and revolutionary changes, both at the conceptual and implementation levels. Indeed, with the global burden of disease shifting from acute to chronic diseases, the philanthropy based model of CSR that responds to short-term ATM needs becomes insufficient to mitigate ATM for chronic conditions. New CSR options, strategic to business revenues and therefore sustained by the private sector, could provide longer-term ATM solutions.

This chapter will first emphasize the importance of ATM and explain why universal ATM has still not been achieved, therefore illustrating the critical role of CSR in this field. The chapter will then discuss the evolution of CSR that aims to increase ATM and provide relevant examples from within and outside the Middle East. Finally, I will present a unique view, supported with practical examples, on how CSR aimed at increasing ATM needs to develop in the Middle East from the current ad hoc philanthropic model to a model that is sustainable to businesses and ensures long-term ATM for chronic diseases.

Access to medicines: definition and critical role

ATM refers to access to the right treatment; treatment that is safe and efficacious, given to the right patient, at the right time, at the right dose and through the right route. How that is accomplished varies, depending on public policies and social values. One common policy approach is based on utilitarian principles (Roberts et al., 2004; Sorenson, 2010; Danzon et al., 2011) and uses a cost-effectiveness perspective and analysis (i.e. getting the biggest bang for the buck). Another perspective is a market-based approach that makes products available for sale to people who can pay the prevailing market prices. The promise of this approach is that market competition, especially among generic medicines, yields to efficient prices, product choice and product quality (Shepard, 2010). A third approach, based on egalitarian values, would preferentially provide subsidized ATM for the patients that are worst off within a population (Roberts and Reich, 2002). In practice, most countries combine these different ethical values in their national policies and approaches to ATM.

The benefits of ATM are numerous: it improves patients' health outcomes, labor and social productivity, and saves costs associated with disease complications and hospitalization. Improving access to existing medicines could save 10 million lives each year worldwide (Department for International Development (DFID), 2004), 4 million of them in Africa and South-East Asia (Hunt, 2007). Unfortunately, there are no published data to quantify these impacts in the Middle East context. The influence of ATM on health outcomes and lifespan is significant. A study lead by Frank Lichtenberg at Columbia University showed that the launch of new chemical entities (innovative medicines) across 52 countries from 1986 to 2000 accounted for about 40 per cent of the two-year increase in life expectancy experienced (Lichtenberg, 2003). More relevant to the Middle East context, the article reported that during the study period countries like Saudi Arabia and Egypt were among the bottom three countries in terms of new drug launches, therefore shedding light on the issue of the delayed launch of innovative medicines in Middle Eastern countries compared with Western or other Asian countries.

The notion of 'sustainable' ATM is becoming more critical to emerging and developing countries (Wirtz et al., 2011) like China, India, Saudi Arabia and the United Arab Emirates (UAE) (Misra and

Khurana, 2008; Popkin, 2008). This is because these countries, which are in an epidemiological transition, suffer from a double burden of diseases: the burden of acute diseases (a trait of developing countries) and the burden of chronic non-communicable diseases (NCDs) like diabetes and many cardiovascular conditions (a trait of developed countries that correlates with modern lifestyle changes). Indeed, in an International Diabetes Foundation (IDF)-sponsored publication about the prevalence of adult diabetes by country/region, the UAE, Saudi Arabia, Bahrain, Kuwait and Oman ranked in the top-10 of countries for both years, 2010 and 2030 (Shaw et al., 2009). Chronic NCDs pose a new and major challenge to emerging middle-income countries compared with the more experienced developed ones. Indeed, middle-income countries, where chronic diseases are already today 'the dominant cause of premature death and lost disability-adjusted life years' (Goroff and Reich, 2010), are still in transition toward the right health-system structure, function and financing which could secure, among other needs, the availability of relevant medicines without imposing financial constraints on patients and their families (Gelders et al. 2005; Mendis et al., 2007; Cameron et al., 2009).

Long-term out of pocket expenditure to treat chronic diseases could lead to what is defined as catastrophic expenditure (if, for example, it exceeds 40 per cent of household disposable income or 10 per cent of total income) or even to impoverishment if the remaining income after drug expenditure is below national poverty levels (Xu et al., 2003). A World Health Organization (WHO and HAI, 2007) study showed that an unskilled government worker in Egypt would pay between 0.1 and 12.6 days' wages for a month's treatment with standard therapies at a private pharmacy. In another example, treatment for depression with fluoxetine cost roughly 12.6 days' wages with the innovator brand drug and two days' wages with the lowest-priced generic substitute. Ensuring equitable access to quality pharmaceuticals is thus a key development challenge and an essential component of health-system strengthening and primary healthcare reform programs throughout the world (WHO, 2011). The United Nations' Millennium Development Goals (MDGs) acknowledge the critical importance of improving access to medicines in setting MDG target 8E, which is: 'in cooperation with pharmaceutical companies, to provide access to affordable essential drugs in developing countries'. Improved access is also a prerequisite to the achievement of several other MDGs, namely MDG 4 (reducing child mortality), MDG 5 (improving maternal health) and MDG 6 (combating Human Immunodeficiency Virus/Acquired Immune Deficiency Syndrome (HIV/AIDS), malaria and other diseases).

Access to medicine: a human right?

The issue of whether ATM is a human right is important to consider because a negative answer means that governments do not have the obligation to provide their citizens with ATM and that access becomes an individual patient responsibility. In this case, through CSR activities businesses could partner with patients and healthcare providers to increase ATM. On the other hand, a positive answer means that governments, which would then transmit the pressure to the private sector (especially to pharmaceutical companies), should secure ATM for their patients. In this case, the private sector's CSR efforts could be more in the form of partnerships and support to governments. This section illustrates some of the views of multinational organizations and Middle Eastern governments on this topic.

The WHO's 1946 constitution states the 'right to the highest attainable standard of health...as a fundamental right of every human being.' This right is continually affirmed within the realm of international agencies. The United Nations' (UN) General Comment 14 says that although states are ultimately accountable for the right to health, 'the private business...[also]...have responsibilities regarding the realization of the right to health'. The UN MDG 8 (Develop a Global Partnership for Development), Target 17 states: 'In cooperation with pharmaceutical companies, provide access to affordable essential drugs in developing countries' (UN, 2005). The international agencies' policies, however, cannot be enforced by law and therefore governments and businesses are meant to implement them through voluntary efforts. In many Middle East countries, the government states explicitly or implicitly that it considers access to healthcare as a human right. The right to healthcare in Saudi Arabia, for example, is referred to in the Basic Law of Saudi Arabia (The Basic Law of Saudi Arabia, Chapter 5, article 31), which declares that: 'The State takes care of health issues and provides healthcare for each citizen.' In practice, most governments issue an 'essential drug list' (EDL) which lists the names of medicines that the government reimburses.

The WHO published the first EDL in 1977 and defined essential drugs as 'those that satisfy the health needs of the majority of the population; they should therefore be available at all times in adequate amounts and in the appropriate dosage form.' National EDL is a practical compromise between the right to access high-quality healthcare and the scarcity of healthcare budgets. It poses the challenge of access to non-listed or non-reimbursed medications and creates an opportunity for CSR activities to support efforts to increase access to these medicines, especially in cases of chronic disease where patients risk catastrophic expenditure. These challenges and opportunities are more relevant to the Middle East, where the 2011 World Medicines Situation publication (WHO, 2011) reported that public-sector availability of generic medicines in the Eastern Mediterranean region is only at 32 per cent and that in countries where patients pay for medicines in the public sector, the average price of generic medicines was around 1.9 times the international reference price. The report also showed that public-sector availability of originator brand medicines is low, and that when these medicines were sold to patients, the average costs were 5.3 times the international reference prices. At the private-sector level, the report valuated the median availability of originator brands at 0 per cent in Syria and Sudan compared with 100 per cent in the UAE. Figure 3.1 shows that none of the indicated Eastern Mediterranean countries has a local cost of treatment (expressed as the number of days that the lowest-paid government worker needs to work to pay for a seven-day course of treatment with ciprofloxacin, 500 mg twice daily) that is lower than a day's wages for both the originator brand and the lowest-priced generic.

What are the major ATM challenges in the Middle East?

The lack of proper ATM could be due to any issue within the pharmaceutical supply chain: from research and development (medicine not discovered), to manufacturing and shipping (trade issues, taxes and intellectual-property protection), to registration, to commercial and pricing strategies, to distribution and sales (high mark-ups, geopolitical events), to prescription and physical access. In many Middle East countries, issues with ATM are mainly due to the high prices – relative to the average patient's purchasing power – of non-reimbursed medicines, and to a lack of discovered medicines (to treat

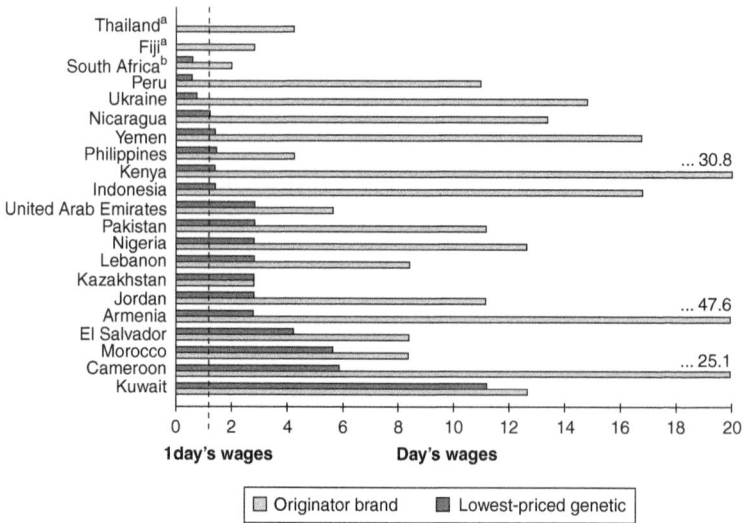

Figure 3.1   Treatment Affordability for Adult Respiratory Infection (expressed as the number of days that the lowest-paid government worker needs to work to pay for a seven-day course of treatment with ciprofloxacin, 500 mg twice daily).

Source: The World Health Organization (2011). 'The World Medicines Situation: Medicines Prices, Availability and Affordability'. (a) Affordability is calculated as 0.1 days' wages. (b) Results of a sub-national survey conducted in Gauteng Province.

diabetes, for example, as all current diabetes medicines slow down but do not prevent or reverse the disease's progression).

Many patients question why pharmaceutical companies do not decrease the prices of their medicines in the Middle East, where patients' purchasing power and per capita gross domestic products are in most cases below the levels of Western countries. In other terms, it is debated why pharmaceutical companies sell their medications at a certain price band rather than applying price differentials depending on local economic indicators, as this could increase both revenues from additional sales and ATM. Price variation is a risk for pharmaceutical companies, mainly for two reasons. The first is international reference pricing (IRP), a practice whereby the low price of a medicine, in Algeria, for example, could be referenced by another country, for example, France. In this case, the pharmaceutical company will have to lower its price in France and then in the countries which reference France and then in the countries that reference the countries that reference France and so on and so forth. Therefore, IRP could potentially lead to major business losses. The second reason is parallel trade, a practice whereby a trader could purchase the medicine from a low-priced country and sell it for a higher price in a rich country, thus gaining the margins that the pharmaceutical company would have earned otherwise. IRP and parallel trade are two main reasons why pharmaceutical companies have historically preferred to sell their medicines at a narrow price band and then in parallel practice philanthropic medicine donations to support patients in need. A major issue with CSR in the form of philanthropic donations is that donations are limited in time and depend on donor revenues and business cycle. Donations are more frequent and suitable in the case of low-income countries where prevailing acute diseases can efficiently be treated with 'acute' donations, but they are less suited to middle-income countries and emerging markets where NCDs are rising, healthcare systems are still transitioning and the average patient's purchasing power is inadequate. A patient lives with diabetes and/or hypertension for decades, but most philanthropic donations do not live as long.

Corporate social responsibility: concepts and evolution in the Middle East

The European Commission defines CSR as 'a concept whereby companies integrate social and environmental concerns in their business operations and in their interactions with their stakeholders on a voluntary basis' (Commission of the European Communities, 2001, 2002). The World Business Council for Sustainable Development (WBCSD) defines CSR as 'the integration of social and environmental values within a company's core business operations and to the engagement with stakeholders to improve the well-being of society' (WBCSD, 2002). A CSR typology developed by Kotler and Lee (2005) classifies the causes of CSR support into: Health (e.g. AIDS prevention/treatment); Safety (e.g. child-proof caps on medicine packaging); Education (e.g. training for doctors on prescription and use of medication); Employment (e.g. training); The Environment (e.g. reduction of harmful emissions, reduced packaging etc.); Community and

Economic Development (e.g. supporting parks, local artists etc.); Other basic Human Needs and Desires (e.g. hunger, homelessness, animal rights, etc.). Kotler and Lee (idem) also suggest a number of methods of support, such as: 'Cash Contributions or Grants; In-kind Contributions e.g. product donations; Transfer of technical and other Know-How and Expertise, Paid Advertising, Publicity & Promotional Sponsorship; Employee volunteering.'

In the following paragraphs we will first reflect on the various views relating to whether a business should engage at all in CSR (or the recently used term 'corporate responsibilities'), and then we will discuss the evolution of CSR activities in the Middle East. We focus on CSR activities that are driven by pharmaceutical companies as these organizations are more involved, knowledgeable and capable of making a difference in improving ATM. Non-pharmaceutical businesses also have a major role to play in increasing ATM, as this chapter will explain in the advocacy and leadership section.

Milton Friedman's conventional view that 'the business of business is business' means that since corporations have a primary moral obligation to maximize economic return for investors, companies should not engage in philanthropy, but rather allow individual investors to determine fund allocation (Friedman, 1970). On the other hand, it is argued that CSR and philanthropy at the company level is more efficient and effective than at the individual level, especially in the case of pharmaceutical companies due to their unique core competency and cost structures. Moreover, business theorists argue that corporate stockholders in their dual role as stockholders and members of the social community share with all others the obligation to act, or to follow a rule governing a class of acts, that will maximize public welfare. For these reasons, stockholders should expect corporate officers to obey the law and advance public welfare while exercising practical business judgments, thus justifying the use of corporate funds to support community projects (Shaw and Post, 1993). The WHO, in its 2004 World Medicines Situation statement, does not point at private corporations for increasing ATM but rather calls for global collaboration to do so: 'Responsibility for increasing access to essential medicines rests with the whole international community. Progress depends on everyone working in partnership to build health systems in developing countries, increase financing, make medicines more affordable, and increase the amount of new medicines developed for diseases affecting developing countries.'

CSR activities to increase ATM in the Middle East started as – and are still prevalent in the form of – charitable donations of medicines and altruistic and voluntary activities (such as 'days of service': the Lilly Day of Service or Hikma's Day against Breast Cancer, 'against obesity' and 'against diabetes'). Such donations and/or activities could make a significant difference to the life of patients with acute and curable diseases, but have a low overall impact on the lives of chronically ill patients. These philanthropic activities also constitute costs to donors and are therefore done at limited levels with a mild impact on the wider public health.

In the past two decades, and in an effort to sharpen CSR's impact on public health, pharmaceutical companies have participated in partnerships with governments and/or loco-regional non-profit organizations in more focused and longer-term public-health initiatives. The International Trachoma Initiative (ITI) is a good example. Trachoma, a bacterial infection of the upper eyelid, is the world's leading cause of preventable blindness. To combat this debilitating disease, Pfizer and the Edna McConnell Clark Foundation formed the ITI in 1998 with the goal of fulfilling the WHO's target of eliminating trachoma by 2020. By 2004, the initiative had reduced the incidence of the disease in children under the age of ten by 90 per cent in Morocco, among many other participating countries, and accomplished a 75 per cent reduction of the overall incidence of the disease in Vietnam and Tanzania. In 2006, trachoma was completely eliminated from Morocco, prompting the ITI to expand the program to a total of 12 countries.

CSR to increase ATM in the Middle East has also taken the form of patient education or training for healthcare providers on disease management. An example is the 2010 agreement signed between the UAE's Ministry of Health and Johnson & Johnson Corporate Citizenship Trust to launch a pilot Primary Health Leadership Program in collaboration with INSEAD (Institut Européen d'Administration des Affaires). This training is intended to meet the specific health needs of the region by focusing on chronic-disease management, which could potentially provide a more long-term impact than short-term donation schemes.

In summary, the most prevalent CSR activities aimed at improving ATM in the Middle East are medicine donations and educational sponsorships, or a mix of both. Although major partnerships and long-term training initiatives have had or could have a stronger public health impact, these activities still constitute 'costs' rather than investment/revenues for pharmaceutical companies and hence are at the mercy of business cycles and have a lower impact on chronic diseases. This portfolio of CSR activities is currently less suitable to the disease profile of many Middle East countries where chronic diseases already constitute a major burden. We argue that while Friedman's view is opposed to conventional CSR activities, innovative CSR strategies that improve ATM while increasing business revenues could satisfy both views and, more importantly, increase ATM in a sustainable way. This approach requires a government's leadership and partnership with the private sector to complete the shift in CSR from being an arbitrary activity and a cost to becoming a sustainable added value to business. As such, CSR could secure long-term ATM for chronic diseases.

Potential CSR strategies for sustainable ATM in the Middle East

Few innovative global partnerships aimed at increasing ATM have gone beyond medicine donation to donating the know-how and/or technology of medicine production. As such, these partnerships constitute a potential opportunity for treating chronic diseases at just the local costs of medicine production. A practical example is the Lilly TB Drug Initiative. Eli Lilly and Co. (Lilly) manufactures two second-line medicines, Capreomycin and Cycloserine, used in the treatment of multi-drug-resistant tuberculosis (MDR-TB). In 2003 Lilly partnered with 15 organizations, including the WHO, Partners in Health, Center for Chronic Diseases of The United States and Purdue University, in a comprehensive effort to improve effective diagnosis, treatment and surveillance of MDR-TB in areas of the world where it is most prevalent. This partnership uniquely integrates disease diagnosis, treatment, access and surveillance, with the transfer of drug manufacturing technology to countries like South Africa and Russia. The new producers can then donate or sell the medicines for very low costs. The partnership integrates many of the components of tuberculosis disease management and is built around the old Chinese proverb: 'give a man a fish and you feed him for a day; teach a man to fish and you feed him for a lifetime.' Indeed, through this partnership, a Russian pharmaceutical company called Biocom, which has received the Lilly technology transfer, has already produced around 800,000 capsules of cycloserine. More detail about this partnership is available at http://www.lillymdr-tb.com/.

Compared with drug donation schemes, the technology transfer model of CSR mitigates the issue of a limited supply of medicines, but it has a few other limitations. It constitutes to the original producer the risk of sharing know-how and intellectual property, the originator company risks market share loss, and to be sustainable the new producer needs to generate revenues to at least balance the costs of production.

To overcome both the sustainability and the financial incentive hurdles, an alternative CSR model to increase ATM should look financially attractive to the medicine producer and at the same time remain affordable to patients based on their ability to pay. Under such a scheme, the older pharmaceutical business model of high prices and minimal price differentials, coupled with philanthropic activities, would be complemented by new options to sell medication to the lower- and middle-class patients at affordable prices. This scheme should also prevent or minimize the risk or impact of IRP and parallel trade to pharmaceutical companies. Since the new scheme has a sales component, some pharmaceutical companies have classified it as alternative pricing models and new business strategies (Lilly, for example), while others have labeled it under CSR to increase ATM (GlaxoSmithKline, for example). In any case, whether selling at fair prices is labeled under CSR or under alternative pricing strategies, we are more interested in this chapter in the consequences of these new approaches, especially the opportunity to increase ATM and impact on the treatment of chronic diseases.

Since 2006, GlaxoSmithKline (GSK) has led an effort to expand sales and treatment in the developing world by selling medicines to patients at different prices based on their ability to pay. The company then expanded this differential or 'tiered pricing' policy, known as 'tearing down the barriers', by offering its medicines at variable prices within the middle-income countries/social classes of India, South Africa and Morocco. Interestingly, GSK not only sells antiretroviral medicines for HIV at lower prices but is now testing its strategy with Avandia, a medicine for diabetes. GSK's new policies are designed to extend its products to less well-off groups at significant discounts and it hopes that distributing a greater volume of sales to a larger share of the population will offset lower prices. Since the beginning of its pilot programs, GSK has identified little parallel trade risk. The company's strategy to minimize parallel trade includes the use of different colors, packaging and branding of the same medicines to distinguish the richer and poorer markets (GlaxoSmithKline Corporate Responsibility Report, 2010). In 2011, GSK, Merck, Johnson & Johnson and Sanofi-Aventis agreed to cut prices through the international vaccine alliance GAVI. GSK announced in 2011 that it was cutting the price of its vaccine for rotavirus by 67 per cent to $2.50 a dose in developing countries.

Other options and strategies, in addition to or besides the GSK-like model, have been explored: the first strategy is 'dual branding'. Under this model, the producing company sells the same molecule in a country or region under two different brands – the original one being priced higher than the other, locally produced, one. Lilly, for example, currently sells two brands of tadalafil in Saudi Arabia: Cialis (original brand) and Snafi, locally produced by Spimaco (Table 3.1).

Another strategy is the patient pharmaceutical card. This card is similar to a credit card and constitutes the basis of a sliding scale discount depending on a patient's ability to pay. A third party or program administrator uses a questionnaire to pre-classify patients based on their ability to pay and then patients get discounts on their purchases accordingly. This scheme has been successfully launched by many pharmaceutical companies in Brazil, for example, where it is easier to do the socio-economic classification, and has proven successful at both increasing ATM and business revenues. Patient cards have the dual benefits of selling to each patient based on his or her ability to pay and keeping product prices non-transparent, hence preventing IRP and parallel trade.

A third strategy is co-pay or co-insurance rebates. Under this scheme a pharmaceutical company partially or fully rebates the patient for the co-pay/co-insurance that he or she incurs upon purchase of a medicine. In this case, the net price paid by the patient is lower and the market price of the medicine remains the same, which prevents IPR and parallel trade. This scheme is regressive,

Table 3.1 Risks and Benefits of CSR Strategies to Increase Access to Medicines

CSR strategies to increase ATM	Description	Risks	Benefits
Philanthropy	Product donation, healthcare, education and so on.	Does not match long-term access needs to treat chronic diseases.	Appropriate for emergency cases (war, earthquakes, etc.) and acute diseases (infectious, accidents, etc.).
Technology transfer	Originator of the drug transfers production know-how to a local producer.	To originator: know-how sharing and loss of market share.	Increase local production of needed medicines.
Tiered pricing	Prices of medicines are adjusted based on local ability to pay.	To originator: potential revenue decrease in other markets through International Reference Pricing.	Prices of medicines are in parity with sub-national economic determinants.
Dual branding	The same molecule is sold under two brands; the branded expensive one and another cheaper equivalent.	Gains in total sales volume might not offset losses in price. Parallel trade of the cheaper brand to other countries.	Cheaper version is at the reach of low-income patients. Opportunity for additional business revenues from the 'new low-income-patients market'.
Patient pharmaceutical card	Patient has a card that makes him/her eligible for discounts, rebates or free goods.	To originator: some patients who are able to pay could subscribe to the system.	Pharmaceutical prices are more or less in parity with each patient's ability to pay.
Co-pay[a] or co-insurance[b] rebates	The producer of the drug rebates patients the co-payment that they incur.	Increases moral hazards.	Mitigates financial hurdle, especially in cases of very-low-income patients and high co-insurance rates.

Table 3.1 (Continued)

CSR strategies to increase ATM	Description	Risks	Benefits
Chronic diseases partnership (CDP)	A local non-profit company charges patients a bundled price for medicines plus other healthcare services.	Limited to the scope of the partnership and involves added logistical costs.	Patients receive healthcare services for lower price. CDP avoids the risk of reference pricing.
Non-profit pharmaceuticals	A local non-profit company produces and sells a medicine at just above cost price.	The producer needs to offset the fixed capital cost and remain solvent under low profit margins.	Local production of the medicine, which is then sold at a relatively low price.
Health financing schemes	Lenders credit low-income patients with small loans to pay for healthcare.	High default rate in some cases. Less effective for chronic care needs.	Provides a financing channel that offsets unexpected, acute healthcare needs.
'Push' strategy to boost R&D	Provides seed money at the beginning of R&D.	The financing institution bears full risk of investment.	Is an effective stimulant for the R&D institution.
'Pull' strategy to boost R&D	Provides a 'trophy' or reward for the R&D institution that discovers a drug.	R&D institutions bear the full risk of conducting research when there could be only one winner.	Pay for outcome/success, which is discovering the target medicine.
Risk-sharing strategies to boost R&D	R&D company and financing institutions share the cost of R&D.	Limited practical experiences with these schemes.	Financial risk is split among financing and R&D institutions.

[a]Pharmaceutical co-pay is a fixed payment that a patient would pay when buying a medicine.
[b]Pharmaceutical co-insurance is a percentage of the total price that a patient has to pay when buying a medicine.

when compared with the more progressive patient card system, as it mitigates costs at the same rate across beneficiaries and does not vary based on a patient's ability to pay. At the same time, this scheme risks increasing moral hazards and the overconsumption of medicines.

A fourth strategy is called chronic diseases partnerships (CDP). This new concept (not applied yet) was introduced in 2010 by Michael Goroff and Michael Reich at Harvard School of Public Health (Goroff and Reich, 2010). The researchers propose a new partnership model which joins pharmaceutical companies with local non-profit organization(s) and local healthcare providers to offer patients, for a certain total price, a bundled medical service including, but not limited to, medicines (physician visits and nursing services, for example). As such, the price of medicine(s) is not transparent to outside purchasers and could not therefore be referenced. At the same time, pharmaceutical companies could control the supply of medicines to the partnership beneficiaries and minimize leakage in case of parallel trade. This partnership model could be a good remedy for integrating the treatment of chronic diseases in emerging countries and the Middle East.

A fifth strategy is the creation of what is called 'non-profit pharmaceutical' companies, which could produce essential medicines and vaccines and sell them to governments and patients at cost prices. Such a model ensures sustainable local access to essential medicines and could help a great deal during times of geopolitical instability and disruption of cross-national distribution channels. An example of a non-profit pharmaceutical organization is OneWorld Health (http://www.oneworldhealth.org/). A major setback for this type of organization is revenue generation and achieving financial sustainability; indeed, the non-profit pharmaceutical will initially fully depend on donor and CSR financing for the facility set-up and production. Later on, the company would need to apply differential pricing to sell at higher prices to the better-off patients. Other challenges for non-profit pharmaceutical companies are achieving a division of labor in partnership with the for-profit pharmaceutical industry, and potentially competing for the business of for-profit companies (Hale et al., 2005).

A sixth strategy would be to encourage the creation of a health financing scheme which could lend patients the money needed to access medicines (chemotherapy drugs and immunosuppressants are good examples). Patients would then gradually pay back the owed amount. Sometimes called micro-financing, if the loan amount is small, this model has proven successful in countries like India, Brazil, Bolivia, Ghana, Morocco and Bangladesh. In contrast to initial assumptions, the experience with micro-loans has shown lower-than-expected payment default rates. It seems that borrowers in this case are ethically committed to return the due amount and want to build a good credit history with the lender as future loans will probably be needed for similar reasons. Articles have reported default rates of 1 per cent in Ghana (Pollio and Obuobie, 2010) to similar or higher anecdotal rates in Bangladesh (Armendariz and Morduch, 2004). Duffau and Pedregal reported that a micro-financing project in Cambodia has enabled the greater utilization of public healthcare, a better perception of the quality of care, and a better capacity for financial anticipation both in healthcare facilities and among the insured (Duffau and Pedregal, 2009). On the other hand, this article showed that self-medication among the insured persisted and that the attitude of poorly paid healthcare workers did not favor the rational use of medicines. In the Middle East, most banks are still skeptical when it comes to implementing micro-financing schemes. Lebanese banks, for example, have only developed a plastic surgery lending system because the 'clientele' for these services are assumed to be of the middle or upper socio-economic classes, and therefore less likely to default on their payments. To alleviate the risk for banks, Middle Eastern private businesses, as part of their CSR strategy, could invest initial funds for healthcare-related lending purposes. Since many Middle East countries follow Islamic laws in finance, the patient could return the loan with no interest or with a minimum extra payment to cover transactional costs. Since micro-financing could open up a new patient base for pharmaceutical companies (the untapped market of low-income patients), lenders could bargain significant discounts for purchased medications and pass along a portion of these discounts to decrease the prices paid by patients and another part could be kept internally to cover operational expenses and default cases. If well designed, lenders, patients and pharmaceutical companies could all be winners under this scheme.

A seventh group of strategies is mostly aimed at boosting the research and development (R&D) process for needed medications rather than impacting on prices. These activities are classified as 'push' and 'pull' strategies. 'Push' strategies aim at alleviating the financial burden for medicine or vaccine discovery: financial support, tax credit, regulatory priority review and partnerships. A limitation of the 'push' strategy is that the cost of each successful medicine discovery could reach tens and hundreds of millions of dollars and so securing the required funds is very challenging. Another limitation of the 'push' strategy is that it is not always obvious which institution is the right one to push, except in a few cases where a pioneering institution is leading cutting-edge research – such as the Buck Institute, which is a global leader in healthy aging research, and Pr. Hajjar's labs at Mount Sinai, which are leading research on gene therapy in heart failure.

'Pull' strategies are based on guaranteeing a profitable market for a medicine or vaccine development, mostly through advanced purchase commitments. A criticism of the 'pull' strategy is that it unfairly gives the entire 'pot of gold' to one 'winner' company even though the winner might have started the R&D process before the start of the race. In this regard, 'pull' strategies create an incentive for R&D companies to be less transparent when sharing information about their research activities. The 'push' and 'pull' strategies also have in common the fact that they do not provide funds 'as you go' in the medicine discovery process. The money is either supplied upfront in insufficient amounts with the 'push' strategy, or after the risk was 100 per cent born by the successful R&D institution in the 'pull' strategy. A risk-sharing approach that alleviates the burden born by both funders and researchers could efficiently help to incrementally build the bridge over the 'valley of death' (translating basic science into clinical research and successful medicine). One risk-sharing strategy in this regard is a 'call option'. Like financial 'calls', this option guarantees low future prices of medicines or vaccines for a premium that is paid during the R&D phase of medicine and vaccine discovery (Brogan and Mossialos, 2006). Besides providing a risk-sharing scheme, call options have the virtue of attracting financial risk-takers and turns a non-profit business that depends on inconsistent financial commitments into a business case with more vested and sustainable interest. In 2011, the Buck Institute for aging research in California pioneered an intriguing scheme of 'venture philanthropy' in which a pro-bono donor co-finances a molecule going through R&D under a scheme that secures him profits if the medicine is successful but no money back if the medicine fails clinical trials (PND, 2011).

Advocacy and leadership to increase ATM

The aforementioned CSR strategies will have better chances of adoption and success if they are supported by dedicated advocacy campaigns. Advocacy groups that are governed by committed leadership have shown success in many cases of access to healthcare. In the USA, for example, the American Association of Retired Persons (AARP) is an advocacy group that lobbies for the interests of US seniors while uninsured citizens, who constitute about 15 per cent of the US population, have no representative advocacy group. At the ATM level, AARP have played a critical role in lobbying the congress for reforms concerning Medicare (an insurance system for seniors), including the passage of the Medicare Prescription Drug, Improvement, and Modernization Act, which in 2003 authorized the creation of Medicare Part D, an entitlement benefit for prescription drugs. On the other hand, the uninsured in the US have remained without any insurance benefits until President Obama's Patient Protection and Affordable Care Act of 2010, but this is currently at the mercy of congressional and presidential elections.

One of the advocacy tactics that proved successful in encouraging CSR is highlighting and benchmarking CSR activities and incentivizing doing more if the opportunity arises. The Access to Medicine Index (http://www.accesstomedicineindex.org/) is an example of this. Founded by the European Agency for Development and Health, the Dutch Ministry of Foreign Affairs, the UK Department for International Development (DFID), the Interchurch Organization for Development Co-operation and Oxfam, the ATM Index assesses and ranks 27 pharmaceutical companies on their efforts to provide ATM, vaccines and diagnostic tests to people living in 88 countries. The index utilizes several criteria and weights for measuring the contribution to ATM. Interestingly, it weights criteria like company management commitment and pricing strategies highly and assigns the lowest weight to medicine donation and philanthropic activities. A similar regional index could be developed to highlight and incentivize ATM activities in the Middle East. The Corporate Social Responsibility Middle East network (CSRmiddleeast.com), along with loco-regional health ministries/authorities and dedicated private-sector companies could constitute the starting platforms for such an initiative. At the institution level, and in a step to make CSR embedded in day-to-day priorities, businesses in the Middle East could develop internal CSR goals and metrics that would be used for management and staff performance reviews.

Recommendations to Middle Eastern governments

The first recommendation that we offer to Middle Eastern governments is to draft and publish clear and transparent national medicine policies, including the government's view on rights to healthcare and its plans to increase ATM (including policies on pricing and reimbursement). Second, we recommend that governments in the Middle East improve their proactive outreach to the private sector and further the discussion of the role of private institutions in healthcare. In many Middle Eastern countries, the private sector is de facto growing in areas where government services are lacking, and such growth could be better supported and tailored if the government plays a positive partnership role.

Third, Middle Eastern governments could issue policies that foster private CSR contributions, such as philanthropic medicine donations, supporting R&D, alternative pricing strategies or any of the aforementioned strategies. It could do so by reviewing tax policies to allow refunds for CSR activities, by matching private contributions to 'pull' and 'push' investments or to set up non-profit pharmaceuticals, and by supporting the banking system with policies that encourage health financing schemes. Fourth, Middle Eastern governments could reform their reimbursement and procurement system to include, besides tenders, contractual and partnership schemes. Although tenders are one of most efficient ways to decrease the prices of procured medicines (Kanavos et al., 2009), they have the drawback of not taking into consideration other potential benefits of contracting, such as: securing patients' and or providers' educational activities; requiring rebates or price reductions in cases of high-volume purchases; or requiring reinvestment of parts of business revenues in local health-system development programs. For instance, the recent deal between the South African government and the pharmaceutical industry, a form of 'social compact', required that instead of decreasing pharmaceutical prices, which would create a wave of IPR and major international revenue losses, the pharmaceutical industry would reinvest part of its revenues in local healthcare programs like First Things First, a voluntary HIV testing, counseling and education campaign. This deal helped the pharmaceutical industry mitigate a potential IPR spiral and at the same time spared the South African government's local healthcare expenditures.

Fifth, Middle Eastern governments could encourage benchmarking and publishing of loco-regional CSR contributions, which has been proven to incentivize private-sector social responsibility, create inter-business competition and translate these responses to actual access to medicine practices (Lee and Kohler, 2010). These publications could be made under a loco-regional CSR partnership and could use platforms like CSR Middle East (csrmiddleeast.org) for publication. It would also be advisable to add to those benchmarks a new CSR performance measurement criterion that reflects the outcome/results of a CSR activity rather than its inputs and goals. Finally, I recommend that governments in the Middle East play the role of a catalyst, as advised under New Public Management principles (Antoun et al., 2011), of public–private and private–private partnerships and proactively engage with the private sector to optimize the conditions for collaborations in healthcare (specifically the case of ATM).

Conclusion

With few exceptions, CSR to increase ATM in most Middle Eastern countries is in the form of philanthropic donations and educational activities. It is perceived by donors as a cost that is external to business activities, as opposed to an internal process that is mainstreamed into core operations or a strategy to create sustainable value for both business and patients. This CSR portfolio is becoming less suitable to treat the regionally more prevalent chronic diseases. This chapter has offered alternative CSR options that incentivize businesses to carry on these activities, therefore making CSR more efficient and sustainable: price differentials with or without dual branding and differential packaging; patient pharmaceutical cards; refund of pharmaceutical co-pay; CDPs; non-profit pharmaceuticals; and health financing. The chapter finally highlighted the role of private-sector advocacy and the proactive role of government as a catalyst and a partner in CSR activities to improve ATM.

Healthcare systems and national pharmaceutical policies vary from one Middle East country to another. Although the aforementioned CSR strategies apply to most Middle Eastern countries, some are more relevant to a system than another. For example, welfare systems, predominantly in the Gulf countries, do not require that patients co-pay for medicines, so a co-pay rebate strategy is less relevant in such a context.

Under an enabling government, the right public–private partnership schemes and a strategic private-sector approach to CSR, ATM through CSR could improve in the Middle East.

References

Antoun J, Phillips F and Johnson T (2011). Post-Soviet Transition: Improving Health Services Delivery and Management. *Mount Sinai Journal of Medicine* 78(3): 436–448.

Armendariz B and Morduch J (2004). *MicroFinance: Where Do We Stand? Financial Development and Economic Growth: Explaining the Links, The Economics of Microfinance* (Cambridge, MA: MIT Press).

The Basic Law of Saudi Arabia, Chapter 5, article 31. http://www.mideastinfo.com/documents/Saudi_Arabia_Basic_Law.htm

Brogan D and Mossialos E (2006). Applying the Concepts of Financial Options to Stimulate Vaccine Development. *Nature Reviews: Drug Discovery* 5: 641–647.

Cameron A, Ewen M, Ross-Degnan D, Ball D and Laing R (2009). Medicine Prices, Availability, and Affordability in 36 Developing and Middle-Income Countries: A Secondary Analysis. *Lancet* 373: 240–249.

Commission of the European Communities (2001). Green Paper Promoting a European framework for Corporate Social Responsibility, Com (2001) 366 final, Brussels, 18th July.

Commission of the European Communities (2002). Communication from the Commission concerning Corporate Social Responsibility: A Business Contribution To Sustainable Development, COM (2002) 347 final, Brussels, 2nd July.

Danzon P, Towse A and Mulcahy A (2011). Pharmaceutical Pricing in Rich and Poor Countries: Setting Cost-Effectiveness Thresholds as a Means to Achieve Appropriate Drug Pricing. *Health Affairs* 30(8): 1529–1538.

Department for International Development (DFID) (2004). Increasing Access to Essential Medicines in the Developing World, London, UK.

Duffau A and Pedregal V (2009). To What Extent Does Non Profit Private Micro Health Insurance Help Improve Public Health Care? *Field Actions Science Reports*, 3. http://factsreports.revues.org/360, accessed 23 April 2012.

Friedman M (1970). The Social Responsibility of Business It to Increase its Profits. *New York Times Magazine*, September 13, 1970, 33, 126.

Gelders S, Ewen M, Noguchi N and Laing R (2005). Price, Availability, and Affordability: An International Comparison of Chronic Disease Medicines. Background Report Prepared for the WHO Planning Meeting on the Global Initiative for Treatment of Chronic Diseases, Cairo Egypt. World Health Organization and Health Action International; Cairo 2006.

GlaxoSmithKline Corporate Responsibility Report (2010). http://www.gsk.com/responsibility/cr-report-2010/access-to-medicines/future-plans/

Goroff M and Reich MR (2010). Partnerships to Provide Care and Medicine For Chronic Diseases: A Model For Emerging Markets. *Health Affairs* December 29: 122206–122213.

Hale V, Woo K and Lipton HL (2005). Oxymoron No More: The Potential of Nonprofit Drug Companies to Deliver on the Promise of Medicines to the Developing World. *Health Affairs* 24(4): 1057–1063.

Hunt P (2007). Human Rights Guidelines for Pharmaceutical Companies in Relation to Access to Medicines. Draft for consultation prepared by the UN Special Rapporteur on the right of everyone to the enjoyment of the highest attainable standard of physical and mental health.

Kanavos PL, Seeley E and Vandoros S (2009). Tender Systems for Outpatient Pharmaceuticals in the European Union: Evidence from the Netherlands, Germany and Belgium. European Commission.

Kotler P and Lee N (2005). *Corporate Social Responsibility: Doing the Most Good for Your Company and Your Cause* (Hoboken, NJ: John Wiley & Sons).

Lee M and Kohler J (2010). Benchmarking and Transparency: Incentives for the Pharmaceutical Industry's Corporate Social Responsibility. *Journal of Business Ethics* 95: 641–658.

Lichtenberg F (2003). The Impact of New Drug Launches on Longevity: Evidence from Longitudinal Disease-level Data from 52 Countries, 1982–2001. NBER Working Paper No. 9754.

Mendis S, Fukino K, Cameron A, Laing R, Filipe A, Khatib O, et al. (2007). The Availability and Affordability of Selected Essential Medicines for Chronic Diseases in Six Low- and Middle-Income Countries. *Bulletin of the World Health Organization* 85(4): 279–288.

Misra A and Khurana L (2008). Obesity and the Metabolic Syndrome in Developing Countries. *The Journal of Clinical Endocrinology & Metabolism* 93(suppl. 1): S9–S30.

Philanthropist News Digest (PND) (2011). Ellen and Douglas Rosenberg Foundation Awards $3.5 Million for Alzheimer's Drug Development. February 4, 2011 accessed at: http://foundationcenter.org/pnd/news/story.jhtml?id=325400003

Pollio G and Obuobie J (2010). Microfinance Default Rates in Ghana: Evidence from Individual-Liability Credit Contracts. Microfinance Information Exchange.   http://www.themix.org/publications/microbanking-bulletin/2010/11/microfinance-default-rates-ghana-evidence-individual-liab

Popkin BM (2008). Will China's Nutrition Transition Overwhelm Its Health Care System and Slow Economic Growth? *Health Affairs* July/August 27(4): 1064–1076. http://content.healthaffairs.org/cgi/reprint/27/4/1064.pdf

Roberts MJ, Hsiao W, Berman P and Reich MR (2004). *Getting Health Reform Right: A Guide to Improving Performance and Equity* (New York: Oxford University Press).

Roberts MJ and Reich MR (2002). Ethical Analysis in Public Health. *The Lancet* 359: 1055–1059.

Shaw B and Post F (1993). A Moral Basis for Corporate Philanthropy. *Journal of Business Ethics* 12(10): 745–751.

Shaw JE, Sicree RA and Zimmet PZ (2009). Global Estimates of the Prevalence of Diabetes for 2010 and 2030. *Diabetes Research and Clinical Practice* 87: 4–14.

Shepard Al (2010). Generic Medicines: Essential Contributors to the Long-Term Health of Society. *IMS Health*. http://www.imshealth.com/imshealth/Global/Content/Document/Market_Measurement_TL/Generic_Medicines_GA.pdf

Sorenson C (2010). *Use of Comparative Effectiveness Research in Drug Coverage and Pricing Decisions: A Six-Country Comparison* (New York: The Commonwealth Fund).

The United Nations (UN) (2005). *Prescription for Healthy Development: Increasing Access to Medicines*. http://www.unmillenniumproject.org/documents/TF5-medicines-Complete.pdf

Wirtz V, Kaplan W, Téllez Y and Ridaura R (2011). Affordable, Quality, Long-Term Care and Pharmacotherapy of Chronic Diseases: A Framework for Low and Middle Income Countries. *Report Commissioned by The Alliance for Health Policy and System Research*. World Health Organization, Geneva.

World Business Council for Sustainable Development (WBCSD) (2002). *The Business Case for Sustainable Development: Making a Difference Towards the Johannesburg Summit 2002 and Beyond*. World Business Council for Sustainable Development, Geneva, Switzerland.

The World Health Organization (WHO) (2011). *The World Medicines Situation: Medicines Prices, Availability and Affordability*. http://www.who.int/medicines/areas/policy/world_medicines_situation/WMS_ch6_wPricing_v6.pdf

The World Health Organization and Health Action International (WHO and HAI) (2007). *Medicine Prices in Egypt; Unpublished Report submitted at the WHO/HAI Post-Medicine Price Survey Workshop*. Cairo, Egypt.

Xu K, Evans DB, Kawabata K, Zeramdini R, Klavus J and Murray CJL (2003). Household Catastrophic Health Expenditure: A Multicountry Analysis. *Lancet* 362: 111–117.

4
CSR: A Cost or an Opportunity for SMEs in the Middle East?

Dima Jamali and Alexandra Tarazi

Introduction

The corporate social responsibility (CSR) debate has to date been very much focused on multinational corporations (MNCs) and driven primarily by a northern agenda. However, CSR is of increasing relevance and concern to small and medium enterprises (SMEs), as suppliers to international companies, as recipients of donor funds and support, and as the critical backbones of economic health and vitality in developed and developing countries (Raynard and Forstater, 2002). While SMEs have long been recognized as important economic players in the developed world, their contributions are only just starting to gain due regard and appreciation in developing countries in the face of the daunting challenges of economic development and global economic integration (Carlos et al., 2007).

SMEs make up 90 per cent of business worldwide and account for 50–60 per cent of employment (Jenkins, 2004; Luetkenhorst, 2004). According to Luetkenhorst (2004), this 90 per cent figure particularly holds true in developing countries. Aside from their strength in numbers, SMEs have established a successful track record globally for their way of building systemic productive capacities, nurturing entrepreneurship and innovation, and serving as attractive ventures for foreign investment (Raynard and Forstater, 2002). Given those facts, any further development of CSR is strongly related to the integration of SMEs in the CSR debate. This is particularly true in developing countries, where firms are mostly alienated from what continues to be perceived as a Western-centric CSR discourse (Jamali and Mirshak, 2007).

Given their important role in generating employment, SMEs are in turn specifically important backbones of economic prosperity in the Middle East. In view of the high unemployment rates across the region (20–25 per cent, but higher for university graduates and women), the creation of sustainable jobs through private-sector growth and investment has been loudly proclaimed as the main challenge facing the region going forward (World Bank, 2009). Yet to date there has been very little research about SMEs and CSR in the Middle East and the peculiar drivers, challenges and opportunities that characterize SME engagement in CSR. This is potentially important if we are to build a solid knowledge base in relation to this important topic.

This chapter considers the drivers, strengths and potential opportunities facing SMEs in their practice of CSR. The chapter begins with a systematic review of the literature pertaining to this topic; there has been a proliferation of writings in recent years on SMEs and CSR, grounded in the realization that SMEs need to adapt to new demands from the market and society pertaining to CSR (Jenkins, 2009). This chapter then examines the CSR practice of two SMEs in the Lebanese context, highlighting how regional SMEs have successfully embraced CSR, and are indeed taking advantage in some cases of the opportunities presented by it. The chapter reveals how SMEs can have a natural affinity to CSR, and that some have progressed to enacting a strategic variety of CSR, linked to core values and competence. The main insights are fleshed out and implications drawn in relation to the SME–CSR debate, particularly in developing countries and in the context of the Middle East region.

Literature review

The nature and orientation of CSR in SMEs

In CSR, the word 'corporate' associated with 'social responsibility' hints at a more significant role expected from 'larger' corporations in the social domain (Jenkins, 2004). For some, the term 'corporate' indeed implies that CSR is only applicable to large enterprises in the form of mission statements, codes of conduct and community projects (Herrmann, 2004). It is therefore not surprising that MNCs have dominated the CSR agenda to date because larger firms are more visible in the public eye and have reputational or brand image risks to consider (Jenkins, 2004). Nevertheless, expecting social involvement solely from MNCs overlooks an important role that can be assumed by SMEs in the social domain (Jenkins, 2004; Luetkenhorst, 2004).

The effective integration of SMEs in the CSR debate has accordingly attracted systematic attention in recent years from governments and international organizations (Jamali et al., 2009). There has also been a proliferation of literature focusing on an exploration of the 'added value' that CSR brings to SMEs in particular (Sarbutts, 2003) and the business case for CSR in SMEs (Raynard and Forstater, 2002; Grayson, 2006). The available literature suggests that SMEs have business practices that reflect elements of CSR, but these do not operate within formalized processes (Fuller and Tian, 2006). According to the literature, many SMEs are unknowingly socially responsible and practice what is referred to as 'silent CSR' or 'sunken CSR' (Jenkins, 2004; Longo et al., 2005; Perrini, 2006; Roberts et al., 2006).

A study conducted by Spence and Lozano (2000) on SMEs in the UK and Spain reveals the important role of owners/managers and the interaction of the personal and social in the context of SMEs, shaping a spontaneous responsible orientation (Spence and Lozano, 2000). Jenkins (2006) similarly suggests that SMEs tend to have a personalized style of management, which does influence their approach to CSR. Beckman, Colwell and Cunningham's study in Chile found that SMEs have been engaged in responsible business practices for many years although these initiatives were not labeled as CSR (Beckman et al., 2009, p. 194). The same conclusion was reached by Vives (2006) in his study investigating 1300 firms across eight countries, which revealed a natural affinity to CSR underlining the personal influence of managers and owners of SMEs.

Research available on the topic to date has therefore successfully captured a number of specifics or peculiarities pertaining to the practice of CSR in SMEs (Jamali et al., 2009). There seems to be consensus in the SME–CSR literature on the following main points: (1) SMEs are already managing a large number of social, economic and environmental impacts, but do not generally use the language of CSR to describe it (Roberts et al., 2006); (2) unlike their MNC counterparts, they do not see CSR in terms of risk management but focus on issues pertaining to employee motivation, retention and community involvement (Jenkins, 2006); (3) SMEs tend to have a personalized style of management with the owners being often insep-arable from the business in terms of values, policies and everyday practice (Murillo and Lozano, 2006); (4) stakeholder relationships for SMEs are more informal and characterized by personal engagement, molding an intuitive responsible orientation (Jenkins, 2006).

Explaining responsible business in SMEs: the drivers

The natural affinity of SMEs to CSR has been explained from differ-ent perspectives. One popular explanation as suggested above is the close entangling of the personal and social in the context of smaller firms, with the values and identity of founders and top managers spilling over to permeate and mold the identity of the organiza-tion (Hannan, 1998; Murillo and Lozano, 2006). Fuller and Tian (2006, p. 287) also affirm that there is an overlap between an owner-manager's personal motives and ethics and the extent to which the business adopts responsible practices. These values and principles are translated into company initiatives that may render the busi-ness responsive to the needs of various stakeholders and responsible vis-à-vis the community.

In addition, religious values specifically are often invoked as impor-tant motivators for CSR engagement in SMEs, given the strong imprint or influence of top managers as explained above. For exam-ple, Azmat and Samaratunge (2009) note that even small-scale indi-vidual entrepreneurs with very limited resources adopt responsible business practices in developing countries despite an often-hostile business environment. They attribute this partially to religious beliefs (2009). Jamali et al. (2009) similarly note that SMEs in developing countries are driven by religious motives and hence take on philan-thropic initiatives as part of their religious responsibility. Vives (2006) also describes ethics and religious values as the 'most consistent reasons' behind CSR practice in SMEs.

Most eloquently, the engagement of SMEs in CSR has been explained from a social capital theory perspective. Social capital refers to intangible assets such as 'reputation, trust, legitimacy, and consen-sus' accumulated through relationships and networks across various spheres of society (Putnam, 1993, 2000; Habisch et al., 2001; Spence et al., 2003, 2004). From this perspective, SMEs engage in CSR in order to nurture their social capital in the form of mutual obligation, reciprocity, trust and respect. SMEs also try to increase their symbolic capital in the form of honor and prestige in the community through socially responsible and ethical behavior (Fuller and Tian, 2006). According to Russo and Perrini (2010), SMEs operate within a fluid structure capitalizing on 'trust, informality, and networking' and invariably seek within this structure to accumulate social capital and reap its benefits, which include improved access to physical, informational and emotional support through various CSR initiatives.

Strengths of SMEs in relation to CSR

SMEs are known to contribute to economic growth and employment and promote social stability (Luetkenhorst, 2004). Their impact is felt on a global scale with their presence making up 90 per cent of businesses worldwide and accounting for 50–60 per cent of employment. The world's least developed countries (LDCs) particularly benefit from SMEs because of their contribution to competitiveness on both national and international levels and their direct influence on gross domestic product (Mezher et al., 2008). According to a recent United Nations Industrial Development Organization (UNIDO) study (Raynard and Forstater, 2002, p. 3), 'SMEs are a seedbed for entrepreneurship development, innovation and risk-taking behavior and provide the foundation for long-term growth dynamics and the transition towards larger enterprises.'

Beyond the economic benefits generated by SMEs, a variety of societal benefits can be added if we account for their informal practice of CSR, or what is commonly referred to as the 'silent CSR'. CSR has been affirmed as an important avenue to improved quality of life and living standards in local communities, catering to the needs of various stakeholders. As suggested above, SMEs have inherent and peculiar characteristics that position them to conduct business responsibly. SMEs have closer ties to the local community than larger enterprises (Spence and Schmidpeter, 2003). They depend on these connections to maintain a good stock of social capital, and ensure their survival and continuity in an increasingly competitive environment (Enderle, 2004; Fuller and Tian, 2006). Moreover, SME managers have more discretion over their business activities than those in charge of larger enterprises do, which allows for personal principles and values to be translated into practice (Spence and Rutherfoord, 2003). According to Jenkins (2006), the managing

Table 4.1 Strengths of SMEs in Relation to CSR

Strengths of SMEs	Description
Manager/owner has great discretion over business practices	SME managers have more discretion over their business than do larger enterprises, allowing for personal principles and values to be translated into practice (Spence and Rutherfoord, 2003).
Flexible decision-making	SMEs are potentially quick on their feet and flexible since they are not burdened with analysts and shareholders fixated by price/earnings ratios (Sarbutts, 2003).
Close ties to community	SMEs can have closer ties to the local community as they are more embedded within their communities (Spence and Schmidpeter, 2003).
Dependence on close community ties	SMEs can benefit from networks accrued within close community relationships. The battle to survive in a competitive environment promotes the need to develop close ties and nurture social capital through responsible relationships (Enderle, 2004).

directors of SMEs have a greater degree of autonomy in how CSR is approached and are helped by their relative freedom in being able to set the agenda. These potential strengths of SMEs in relation to CSR are summarized in Table 4.1.

Challenges of SMEs in relation to CSR

While some of the inherent characteristics of SMEs may create a strong potential and inclination to conduct business responsibly, there are parallel concrete challenges which may hinder the enactment of CSR by SMEs. For example, SMEs are often constrained by time and resources and are particularly burdened by the urgent need to address priorities such as 'improving the quality of technology, management and marketing' (Raynard and Forstater, 2002, p. 65). In addition, SMEs may lack the necessary expertise to improve their formal practice of responsible business conduct (UNIDO, 2002). This is due to the lack of appropriate best practices and information adapted to SMEs and the lack of support networks to establish CSR priorities, discuss action plans, link CSR to financial performance and provide guidance to SMEs on CSR performance and impact assessments (Roberts et al., 2006). Also, as mentioned above, SMEs tend to practice CSR intuitively, thus steering away from strategic CSR, which is more sustainable and long-term given that it is integrated/linked to the strategy and goals of the organization. In addition, the lack of pressure exercised by consumers and price competition may hinder SMEs from investing in CSR (Raynard and Forstater, 2002).

Moreover, a salient constraint in relation to SME engagement in CSR continues to revolve around the language of CSR itself, which is not adapted to the specifics of SMEs and hence serves to alienate SMEs from the evolving CSR discourse. Notably, Jenkins (2004) argues that 'SMEs are frequently seen as a problem within the CSR debate because of their failure to engage with it. An alternative interpretation is that it is the CSR debate that is the problem, because of its failure to engage SMEs.' In a study of 24 SMEs in the UK it was found that rather than using the term CSR, SMEs defined responsible business behavior according to various practices, such as 'community involvement' or 'work-life balance' (Jenkins, 2006). Some would argue that the broad definition of CSR itself can cause confusion among SMEs that feel pressured to tackle issues as varied as 'animal rights, corporate governance, environmental management, corporate philanthropy, stakeholder management, labor rights, and community development' (Blowfield and Frynas, 2005, p. 501). Conill et al. (2000) argued that the term CSR should be replaced with language that is more adaptable to SMEs. These potential challenges and constraints are summarized below in Table 4.2.

SMEs and CSR in developing countries

In addition to the constraints mentioned above, SMEs in the developing world are likely to face further complexity in their CSR practice and an exacerbated set of challenges that stem from the characteristics of governance and the business environment of developing nations. For example, Azmat and Samaratunge (2009) researched responsible behavior of SMEs in developing countries, noting exacerbated challenges stemming from the prevalence of corruption, the regulatory quality, and the rule of law (Azmat and Samaratunge, 2009, p. 443). Corruption, for example, is known to negatively

Table 4.2 Challenges of SMEs in Relation to CSR

Challenge	Description
Time and resources	Limited amount of time and resources to allocate to CSR initiatives with SMEs particularly burdened by the urgent need to address salient business priorities (Raynard and Forstater, 2002).
Lack of appropriate expertise and support	SMEs may lack the necessary expertise to make improvements to their responsible business conduct due to the lack of appropriate best practices, information and support networks adapted for SMEs (Roberts et al., 2006).
Dichotomy between economic and social goals	SMEs' CSR initiatives tend to represent a dichotomy between economic and social goals, steering away from strategic CSR, where philanthropic contributions are often not aligned with business operations (Jamali et al., 2009).
Lack of consumer pressure	Lack of pressure exercised by consumers and price competition may hinder SMEs from investing in CSR initiatives (Raynard and Forstater, 2002).
Broad definition of CSR	There remains confusion as to which specific issues and stakeholders should be addressed due to the broad definition of CSR (Blowfield and Frynas, 2005).
Difficulty in understanding CSR terminology	The terminology used to define CSR can pose problems for SMEs. Many SMEs express difficulty in understanding the terms and language of CSR (Conill et al., 2000; Jenkins, 2006).

affect economic and social development. Typically, with corruption, resources are less equally distributed among the population with 'patron-client' relationships prioritizing preferred groups (World Bank, 2005). Regulation in developing countries is also often characterized as weak with insufficient mechanisms to enforce contracts or promote abidance to set standards (Azmat and Samaratunge, 2009). Many developing countries also have no consumer protection laws (Azmat and Samaratunge, 2009). Finally, due to poor regulation and corruption, people in developing countries often do not have any trust in rules and often complain of discretionary rule implementation (Azmat and Samaratunge, 2007).

The Middle East and North Africa (MENA) region shares many of the characteristics of poor governance described above, which are likely to spillover and affect the CSR practice of private corporations of all sorts including SMEs. As aptly presented by a recent World Bank report (2009) private-sector development is impeded by weak and opaque public-sector governance, limited accountability, transparency and participation and the predominance of various forms of rents and privileges. According to the World Bank's MENA Regional Economic Update Report, 'Key problems of the business environment in MENA include policy and regulatory uncertainty and discretion in implementing reforms, which prevent a level playing field for all firms and encourage the pursuit of privileged access' (World Bank, 2010). While reforms have accelerated in recent years, wide policy gaps persist in most countries and in critical policy areas, and private investment rates in MENA have on average been less responsive to reforms than elsewhere (World Bank, 2009).

The business environment in the MENA region is also characterized by the predominance of family owned businesses (Al Masah Capital Limited, 2011). Roughly 5000 medium- to large-sized family firms exist in the Middle East with net assets totaling US$600 billion, accounting for 75 per cent of the private-sector economy and employing an estimated 70 per cent of the labor force (Al Masah Capital Limited, 2011). These family businesses go back many generations and are closely intertwined with the development of the region. Commonly in the family business sector, kinship and family provide guarantees of loyalty and communal solidarity, shaping the whole gamut of social relationships (Al Masah Capital Limited, 2011). Similarly, the Lebanese business environment has been described as not conducive to long-term business success because of poor national policies, cumbersome bureaucracy, inefficient administrative procedures, a weak judicial sector, lack of contract enforcement and non-comprehensive labor laws which invariably impede business growth, development and innovation (Mezher et al., 2008). These contextual realities should therefore be kept in mind as we delve into the analysis of the CSR practices of the SMEs in question in the Lebanese context.

Case study: CSR in Lebanese SMEs

Lebanon is home to a wide array of SMEs that make up 98 per cent of the country's businesses; largely family owned, they account for 72.4 per cent of employment (ESCWA Report, 2001; Mezher et al., 2008). The prevalence of SMEs in Lebanon makes it essential to understand the specific strengths and challenges they face in implementing CSR. Some of these areas were identified through in-depth, semi-structured interviews with the top management of two medium-sized Lebanese firms, Segenius and Muhanna Group. The in-depth interviews probed around the four key themes related to CSR in the Lebanese SME context. These themes are: (a) the drivers of responsible business; (b) the formalization of CSR; (c) CSR priorities; and (d) barriers, strengths and opportunities presented through CSR. The fieldwork was complemented by an analysis of company websites and relevant documents pertaining to CSR. The highlights of these two cases studies are fleshed out below, providing very interesting insights into the practice of CSR in SMEs in Lebanon and in the context of the Middle East region more broadly.

Company overviews

Segenius is a medium-sized company consisting of 30 employees. It provides consultancy services in the fields of telecom and renewable energy and has been in operation for eight years. Muhanna Group is also a medium-sized company with 30 employees. It provides actuarial consultancy to businesses, governments, trade unions and various institutions, and has been in operation for 26 years. Both companies are owned by independent entrepreneurs. The table below provides a general description of the companies (Table 4.3).

Drivers of responsible business

In general, both companies appreciated the importance of CSR and were familiar with its language, although they did not feel the urge to label what they were doing as CSR. The respondents from both Segenius and Muhanna Group described CSR as a tool for engagement to improve the quality of life of the community. In other words, both companies appreciated the embedded-ness, interconnectedness and interdependencies of the business and its surrounding

Table 4.3   Company Description

Company	Segenius	Muhanna Group
Number of employees	30	30
Type of business	Medium-sized	Medium-sized
Years in operation	6	26
Sector description	Provides consultancy services in the fields of telecom and renewable energy.	Provides actuarial consultancy to businesses, governments, trade unions and various other institutions.
Interviewee position	Public relations manager	Owner/managing director
Ownership	Independent entrepreneur	Independent entrepreneur
Management	Founder/chairman/CEO; financial manager; technology manager; marketing manager	Founder/managing director

community and the need for proactivity and joint effort to address relevant social and environmental concerns. CSR was also recognized by Segenius as a way to provide clients with the very best quality services and cater to their needs. This SME therefore recognizes that the success of the business depends on support and interaction with different stakeholder groups, particularly customers, and CSR was conceived as a way to reduce risks in the eyes of customers. Muhanna Group specifically stated that CSR should involve full engagement with the community beyond mere philanthropy. This engagement, according to the owner, helps to improve the exchange of relevant information and bolster the trustworthiness of the firm in the eyes of its stakeholders. The Muhanna founder/manager pointed out that they are well known and respected in the community because of their CSR initiatives, referring indirectly to symbolic capital and the 'credit of renown' through symbolic authority, prestige and improved reputation (Fuller and Tian, 2006).

In other words, for Segenius' public relations manager, CSR has public relations value and it is likely to increase trust in the company's services if the business markets itself as a responsible and ethical company. The other important driver that this manager referred to pertained to improved employee motivation and retention, in the sense that CSR in the workplace and the community helps motivate employees and creates a sense of common identity and joint collective effort and engagement. The owner-manager of Muhanna Group was driven morally to contribute to society and believed that his business had a duty to give back as much as it could to society. The ethical/religious motive was strongly accentuated by this manager, but this moral motivation did not in any way attenuate appreciation of the other business-related drivers, including the importance of community engagement to improve relationships with stakeholders and garner social capital. The drivers cited by both managers are consistent with what is reported in the literature, and generally point to an inclination among these SMEs to consider CSR as an opportunity rather than a cost or a threat. This will be dwelled upon further in the following sections.

CSR formalization

Segenius and Muhanna Group both accorded semi-fixed budgets for the support of their own non-profit organizations. Both companies were interested in formalizing their commitment to responsible business through a code of conduct or a CSR policy, but did not believe that it was a prerequisite for responsible behavior. Neither company had a specific CSR unit or division. In the case of Muhanna Group, CSR was primarily led by the owner/managing director; therefore, CSR was shaped according to his vision, objectives and beliefs. In the case of Segenius, responsibility for CSR was shared between the founder/chairman/CEO and three other managers in various departments. While the principles and values of the founder permeated the entire business, responsible initiatives were jointly steered and managed by this group, which invariably reached for input and support from across the organization. None of the companies conducted social or environmental audits or impact assessments on their responsible practices. Segenius did abide by certain business standards, but did not perform any social or environmental audits on its operations. However, it published the goals and achievements of its non-profit organization online. In addition, Muhanna Group produced annual reports on the activities of its non-profit organization, highlighting its initiatives and beneficiaries.

In other words, in line with the existing literature, the companies did not exercise an entirely formalized approach to CSR, yet they had made some progress in the way of institutionalization through creating their own non-profit organizations and allocating a semi-fixed budget rather than sporadically providing donations to various non-governmental organizations (NGOs). Furthermore, both companies provide information on their organization's objectives and achievements on dedicated websites, while Muhanna Group also produces an annual report.

CSR priorities

Community. Segenius's founder created his own NGO, Amour et Partage, which cares for the elderly in marginalized and impoverished areas by providing them with shelter. A home housing more than 30 people was built in the community where the beneficiaries grew up and with which they were familiar. The building incorporates the necessities for elderly care, including a clinic to cater to any medical needs. More than 50 people have resided in the nursing home since its inception in 2003 and 15 people live there permanently. The NGO is currently involved in raising additional funds to build another home to accommodate more elderly people deprived of safe shelter. The NGO is sponsored by company funds as well as by private donations. All employees, ranging from the secretary to the CEO, volunteer time with the NGO, which ensures long-term engagement at the heart of the community between its various constituencies in a joint effort to address a salient and important social issue pertaining to securing care and attention for the elderly.

Muhanna Group is also fully engaged with a particular social issue, namely education. It established its own non-profit organization, the Muhanna Foundation, to magnify its impact in this respect. The owner-manager stated that the foundation was created in the early days of the establishment of the company and is almost entirely funded by company profits. Its function is to provide actuarial education and continuing education for professionals living in underdeveloped countries, particularly in the Arab world, in the fields of social security, pensions, healthcare, insurance and supervision. It organizes workshops, conferences and seminars on these topics and grants three different types of diplomas: Actuarial Sciences, Social Insurance and Healthcare. It also provides scholarships to students from eight countries across the Middle East who are seeking to pursue a career in actuarial services. In addition, Muhanna Group holds annual blood drive campaigns in alliance with the Lebanese Red Cross. It also finances annually a research project of interest and benefit to the general public and publishes the study online.

Environment. Segenius provides consultancy on renewable energy in the construction sector, which it views in the broader context of making available an environmentally responsible service to Lebanon. Muhanna Group encourages carpooling among its employees by setting up a system based on employees' schedules and locations. Although the environment is not very high on the CSR agenda of either company, it is nevertheless recognized as important and accounted for as part of what seems to be a rounded holistic conception of CSR.

Workplace. Segenius provides its employees with paid hours to participate weekly in volunteer work either for the company's NGO or for another of their choice. A healthy work–life balance is also prioritized, doing away with the rigid nine-to-five work schedule. However, regular training workshops for employees are not emphasized, and are generally organized according to need. Muhanna Group, on the other hand, is committed to ensuring the professional development of its employees. Training workshops in actuarial services are frequently organized and regularly provided. In addition, the owner-manager encourages his employees to volunteer paid working time at the non-profit organization. This, according to the manager, secures a healthy break from the normal work routine, while also ensuring regular employee engagement with the NGO and with the particular social issue that they have set out to address jointly.

Marketplace. Since they are in the services sector, these companies do not engage regularly with suppliers and therefore have not accorded attention to the creation of sustainable and responsible practices across the supply chain. However, both companies emphasize the need for accountability and transparency in all of their operations to avoid corruption and take measures to promote internal and external transparency through improved internal and external communication and better reporting.

Barriers to CSR

Segenius cited insufficient financial resources and time as barriers to CSR endeavors. While the company supports its NGO financially, it still needs and seeks the support of private donors to ensure the continuity of its CSR efforts in this domain; the manager commented also in this respect on the necessity of governmental support, recognition and tax incentives for SMEs involved in CSR work. Muhanna Group, on the other hand, stated that neither financial resources nor time were barriers to supporting their non-profit foundation or toward other responsible initiatives such as catering to employee capacity building. The owner/managing director affirmed that the company was prepared to sacrifice profit to support its non-profit organization and employee training programs fully. The manager recognized the need for a holistic approach to conducting business, which prioritizes human well-being, not profits, and which seeks to add value in the broadest sense, not only through classical business transactions. This is not in any way intended to mean that challenges do not exist for the Muhanna manager, but that we need to find a way to look beyond costs and constraints, and identify opportunities for giving, helping and innovation as part of a shared existence.

Strengths in relation to CSR

The SME managers cited many of the strengths mentioned in the SME literature, including embedded-ness and strong ties to the community which help them stay in tune with community needs and demands. This was identified as a major strength of both companies with regard to developing and implementing CSR initiatives. Both companies also benefited from the strong vision, moral orientation and philosophy of their founding members, although this influence was more strongly felt in the case of the Muhanna Group, where the ethical/religious motivations of the founder were strongly emphasized. Both SMEs benefited as well from flexible decision-making and a level of autonomy in implementing CSR, which was complemented by great sensitivity to the needs of the community and an unwavering commitment to engage and make a difference.

Opportunities in relation to CSR

It is interesting to note that in both cases there was more emphasis on the opportunities presented by CSR than on the costs, challenges and constraints. Perhaps the fact that a responsible business orientation had been voluntarily embraced by both SMEs from early on accounts for this appreciation of CSR and the opportunities it presents. For example, both managers recognized the intangible benefits accrued through responsible initiatives, including reciprocity, trust, respect, prestige and visibility in the community. Both SMEs, in other words, implicitly recognized the link between CSR and the accumulation of social capital. Both managers also alluded to employee motivation as an important benefit or opportunity presented through the practice of CSR. In other words, CSR is perceived as a strategy to enhance different forms of engagement and cooperation inside and outside the organization.

Both SMEs also managed to identify a particular societal need or social issue in the community and focused their engagement around it. This is noteworthy in the sense that it diverges from common CSR trends reported in the SME literature, which tend to be sporadic, ad hoc and not strategized in a systematic way over the long term. Both companies have also made good strides in catalyzing the commitment to CSR across the organization through volunteering and other initiatives, which is also something that is not commonly reported in the SME literature. Interestingly, one of the SMEs (Muhanna Group) managed to identify and address a social issue that links to its core expertise in actuarial services, aligning its business operations with its investment in society. The SME was successful in connecting its CSR to its business strategy, which, according to Porter and Kramer (2006, 2011), maximizes business opportunities to benefit society by drawing on a core competence and maximizing the potential for creating shared value.

Discussion and implications for SME–CSR practice in the Middle East

The findings presented through the case studies of the Lebanese SMEs and their orientation to CSR confirm what is commonly reported in the CSR–SME literature, namely that the close entangling of the personal and the social in the context of SMEs, the strong influence of founders/owners and top managers, the flexibility in relation to decision-making, the greater sense of embedded-ness within communities and strong ties forged with the community provide an important roadmap in the CSR domain. In other words, these Lebanese SMEs share the same spontaneous affinity to CSR, and their CSR is grounded in a crystallized ethos system and values pertaining to trust, humanity and integrity.

Consistent with previous literature, our findings also suggest that SMEs focus their CSR practice on social issues that are close to home (i.e. relevant to their business or immediate community), as in, for example, work–life balance internally or employee training and development. Externally they also focus on the vexing issues that lie at the heart of the community, such as elderly care or improved education and educational opportunities. In other words, their approach to CSR is more customized (less generic) than large businesses, and they exert consistent efforts both internally and externally to refine their choices of causes and interventions that would add value to their internal and external stakeholders.

The findings also suggest that the SMEs selected do not use the difficult surrounding business environment as an excuse or justification for not engaging in CSR. Rather, both SMEs exhibit a full appreciation of the benefits of CSR, with a focus on opportunities rather than constraints and costs. Both SMEs echoed views that reflect an appreciation of what is commonly known as the business case for CSR – improved image and visibility in the community, enhanced risk management, the accumulation of social capital (trust, respect, reciprocity) and increased employee motivation. In other words, for them the CSR agenda need not necessarily be treated as a threat, a cost or burden but rather as a potential opportunity.

This finding is particularly interesting and has potential implications for SMEs across the Middle East, in the sense that the common complaints from SMEs when it comes to CSR revolve around cost and a non-conducive business environment. However, the two cases highlighted here suggest that SMEs can indeed pursue added value and competitive advantage through an appreciation of the benefits of CSR and a positive inclination to look for opportunities for differentiation and innovation through CSR engagement. What is also worth noting is that one of the SMEs interviewed also managed to forge a strategic approach to CSR by leveraging their core competence and linking their CSR interventions to their core strategy and goals.

In this respect, it would be fair to conclude that SMEs are indeed capable of riding the CSR wave, and adding value both internally and externally. This necessitates a change in mindset and a positive orientation, focusing on opportunities and benefits in the context of a clear value system. To say that we cannot expect SMEs to engage in CSR is far-fetched, since even small companies can, through soul searching and their close ties to their community, identify various avenues and paths to address social issues that are relevant to the stakeholders and the community, even on a small and more limited scale than large corporations. These cases also make it clear that CSR can take significant leaps forward when a company benefits from the championing and support of top management.

Conclusion

This chapter has provided a comprehensive summary and consolidation of the literature on CSR and SMEs. It has also offered fresh empirical insights from the Lebanese context pertaining to the CSR practice of local SMEs. While recognizing that the findings are not necessarily generalizable, this chapter has nevertheless identified a window of opportunity for SMEs in the domain of CSR, through a focus on leveraging their strengths and their embedded-ness in the community to identify social issues that can be addressed jointly through proactive action and engagement. Through concrete examples, the cases provide insights into how SMEs can practice CSR and what the important ingredients are for success in this respect. These include an unwavering commitment from top management, value-based management, a sensitized orientation to internal and external stakeholders, along with a focus on the benefits and opportunities presented through CSR. Even in the most difficult business environment, and with limited resources, SMEs can identify a path and mechanisms to make a positive difference in the lives of their employees and their community. CSR projects need not be large in scale or grandiose, but can still touch many lives in a positive way. While each SME may not have a significant impact individually, their aggregated impact can be considerable. This is an important message that we wish to leave the reader with, and we hope that it will serve as a catalyst for the active involvement in CSR by SMEs across the region.

References

Al Masah Capital Limited (2011) 'MENA Family Businesses: The Real Power Brokers?', MENA Family Businesses Report. Available at: http://www.almasahcapital.com/uploads/media/MENA_Family_Businesses_Report__17-Apr-11_.pdf

Azmat, F. and R. Samaratunge (2007) 'Responsible Entrepreneurism in Developing Countries', *presented at the AIB (UK & Ireland) Annual Conference at King's College London.* London, 13–14 April 2007.

Azmat, F. and R. Samaratunge (2009) 'Responsible Entrepreneurship in Developing Countries: Understanding the Realities and Complexities', *Journal of Business Ethics*, 90 (3), 437–452.

Beckman, T., A. Colwell and P.H. Cunningham (2009) 'The Emergence of Corporate Social Responsibility in Chile: The Importance of Authenticity and Social Networks', *Journal of Business Ethics*, 86 (2), 191–206.

Blowfield, M. and J.G. Frynas (2005) 'Setting New Agendas: Critical Perspectives on Corporate Social Responsibility in the Developing World', *International Affairs*, 81 (3), 499–513.

Carlos, M., V. Martos and F. Torraleja (2007) 'Is Family Business More Socially Responsible: The Case of GRUPO CIM', *Business and Society Review*, 112 (1), 121–136.

Conill, J., A. Arino, D. Garcia-Marza, E. Garrido, E. Gonzalez, M. Llofriu and C. Soriano (2000) 'The Ethical Dimension of Corporate Culture in the Regional Community of Valencia', *ETNOR- Economia*, 3, 2–36.

Enderle, G. (2004) 'Global Competition and Corporate Responsibility of Small and Medium- Sized Enterprises', *Business Ethics: A European Review*, 13 (1), 51–63.

ESCWA Report (2001) 'The Role of SMEs in National Economies in East Asia', ESCWA.

Fuller, T. and Y. Tian (2006) 'Social and Symbolic Capital and Responsible Entrepreneurship: An Empirical Investigation of SME Narratives', *Journal of Business Ethics*, 67 (3), 287–304.

Grayson, D. (2006) 'Inspiring Smaller Firms With the Responsible Business Mindset', in M. Epstein and K. Hansen (eds), *The Accountable Corporation: Corporate Social Responsibility* (Praeger, London), pp. 279–298.

Habisch, A., H.P. Meister and R. Schmidpeter (2001) *Corporate Citizenship as Investing in Social Capital* (Logos-Verlag, Berlin, Germany).

Hannan, M. (1998) 'Rethinking Age Dependence in Organizational Mortality: Logical Formulations', *American Journal of Sociology*, 104 (1), 126–164.

Herrmann, K.K. (2004) 'Corporate Social Responsibility and Sustainable Development: The European Union Initiative as a Case Study', *Indiana Journal of Global Legal Studies*, 11 (2), 205–232.

Jamali, D. and R. Mirshak (2007) 'Corporate Social Responsibility (CSR): Theory and Practice in a Developing Country Context', *Journal of Business Ethics*, 72 (3), 243–262.

Jamali, D., M. Zanhour and T. Keshishian (2009) 'Peculiar Strengths and Relational Attributes of SMEs in the Context of CSR', *Journal of Business Ethics*, 87 (3), 355–377.

Jenkins, H. (2004) 'A Critique of Conventional CSR Theory: An SME Perspective', *Journal of General Management*, 9 (4), 55–75.

Jenkins, H. (2006) 'Small Business Champions for Corporate Social Responsibility', *Journal of Business Ethics*, 67 (3), 241–256.

Jenkins, H. (2009) 'A "Business Opportunity" Model of Corporate Social Responsibility for Small- and Medium-Sized Enterprises', *Business Ethics: A European Review*, 18 (1), 21–36.

Longo, M., M. Mura and A. Bonoli (2005) 'Corporate Social Responsibility and Corporate Performance: The Case of Italian SMEs', *Corporate Governance*, 5 (4), 28–42.

Luetkenhorst, W. (2004) 'Corporate Social Responsibility and the Development Agenda-The Case for Actively Involving Small and Medium Enterprises', *Intereconomics*, Available at: http://www.springerlink.com/index/R4Q5T656M40178G1.pdf [Accessed 26 August 2011].

Mezher, T., R. El-Saouda, W. Nasrallah and M. Al-Ajam (2008) 'Entrepreneurship in Lebanon: a model for successes and failures', *International Journal of Arab Culture, Management and Sustainable Development*, Available at: http://inderscience.metapress.com/app/home/contribution.asp?referrer=parent&backto=issue,3,7;journal,3,3;linkingpublicationresults,1:121242, [Accessed 30 August 2010].

Murillo, D. and J. Lozano (2006) 'SMEs and CSR: An Approach to CSR in their Own Words', *Journal of Business Ethics*, 67 (3), 227–240.

Perrini, F. (2006) 'SMEs and CSR Theory: Evidence and Implications from an Italian Perspective', *Journal of Business Ethics*, 67, 305–316.

Porter, M. and M. Kramer (2006) 'Strategy & Society: The Link Between Competitive Advantage and Corporate Social Responsibility', *Harvard Business Review*, 84 (12), 78–92.

Porter, M. and M. Kramer (2011) 'Creating Shared Value', *Harvard Business Review*, 89 (1/2), 62–77.

Putnam, R. (1993) *Making Democracy Work: Civic Traditions in Modern Italy* (Princeton University Press, Princeton, NJ).

Putnam, R. (2000) *Bowling Alone: The Collapse and Revival of American Community* (Simon and Schuster, New York, NY).

Raynard, P. and M. Forstater (2002) *Corporate Social Responsibility: Implications for Small and Medium Enterprises in Developing Countries* (United Nations Industrial Development Organization, Vienna, Austria).

Roberts S., R. Lawson and J. Nicholls (2006) 'Generating Regional-Scale Improvements in SME Corporate Responsibility Performance: Lessons from Responsibility Northwest', *Journal of Business Ethics*, 67 (3), 275–286.

Russo, A. and F. Perrini (2010) 'Investigating Stakeholder Theory and Social Capital: CSR in Large Firms and SMEs', *Journal of Business Ethics*, 91 (2), 207–221.

Sarbutts, N. (2003) 'Can SMEs "Do" CSR? A Practitioner's View of the Ways Small- and Medium-Sized Enterprises are Able to Manage Reputation through Corporate Social Responsibility', *Journal of Communication Management*, 7 (4), 340–347.

Spence, L.J., A. Habisch and R. Schmidpeter (2004) *Responsibility and Social Capital: The World of Small and Medium Sized Enterprises* (Palgrave Macmillan, Houndmills, UK/New York, NY).

Spence, L.J. and J.F. Lozano (2000) 'Communicating about Ethics with Small Firms: Experiences from the U.K. and Spain', *Journal of Business Ethic*, 27 (1–2), 43–53.

Spence, L.J. and R. Rutherfoord (2003) 'Small Business and Empirical Perspectives in Business Ethics: Editorial', *Journal of Business Ethics*, 47 (1), 1–5.

Spence, L.J. and R. Schmidpeter (2003) 'SMEs, Social Capital and the Common Good', *Journal of Business Ethics*, 45 (1–2), 93–108.

Spence, L.J., R. Schmidpeter and A. Habisch (2003) 'Assessing Social Capital: Small and Medium Sized Enterprises in Germany and the UK', *Journal of Business Ethics*, 47 (1), 17–29.

United Nations Industrial Development Organization (UNIDO) and The World Summit on Sustainable Development (2002) *Corporate Social Responsibility Implications for Small and Medium Enterprises in Developing Countries*, Vienna. Available at: http://www.unido.org/fileadmin/user_media/Publications/Pub_free/Corporate_social_responsibility.pdf [Accessed 4 May 2011].

Vives, A. (2006) 'Social and Environmental Responsibility in Small and Medium Enterprises in Latin America', *Journal of Corporate Citizenship*, 21, 39–50.

World Bank (2005) 'A Better Investment Climate for Everyone', World Development Report, Washington, DC.

World Bank (2009) 'From Privilege to Competition: Unlocking Private-Led Growth in the Middle East and North Africa', MENA Development Report. Available at: http://www-wds.worldbank.org/external/default/main?pagePK=64193027&piPK=64187937&theSitePK=523679&menuPK=64187510&searchMenuPK=64187283&theSitePK=523679&entityID=000333037_20091124234258&searchMenuPK=64187283&theSitePK=523679

World Bank (2010) 'MENA Regional Economic Update: Recovering from the Crisis, April 2010'. Available at: http://go.worldbank.org/TMG48JN8C0

5
Socially Responsible Employee Management: Case Studies from Saudi Arabia and Lebanon

Marian Eabrasu and Akram Al Ariss

Introduction

A recent mainstream approach to corporate social responsibility (CSR) research is to provide a unique set of ethical principles and standards, such as the *Interfaith Declaration on Business Ethics, Global Compact, ISO 26000*, which are designed to be applicable worldwide to deal with the eternal issue of cultural differences and with the subsequent problem of 'incomprehension' which results (Moran et al., 2007). Yet such global approaches to social responsibility are limited by their own generality. The widely accepted interpretations of CSR are necessarily diluted. In addition, they veil the view of the cultural specificities of CSR strategies and various forms of informal CSR practices. Hence, instead of working on a diluted idea of social responsibility, we propose in this chapter to focus on informal CSR practices in a medium enterprise (ME) within the context of the Middle East. MEs are described as multitasking, cash-limited, locally operating and dependent on internal sources to finance growth (Spence, 1999; Tilley, 2000).The Middle East is a region of particular interest and significance with regard to the understanding of CSR challenges in human resource management (Jamali et al., 2006; Jamali and Abdallah, 2009; Abbas, 2010; Sidani and Jamali, 2010). However, we find very little regarding the contexts of Saudi Arabia and Lebanon in management and organizational literature (Bozionelos, 2009; Al Ariss, 2010).

We propose to take the examples of Assad Said Company (ASC), operating in Saudi Arabia (KSA), and the Window Cleaning Company

(WCC) in Lebanon. With more than 1500 employees and projects in KSA and across the Gulf region, ASC specializes in contracting services. WCC is a professional cleaning business and has 453 employees. Neither company has yet organized human resources management (HRM) activities. Interviews conducted with the presidents of the two companies and the key managers, coupled with observation notes taken regarding their working contexts, show how personnel administration offers original venues for care and compassion in socially responsible HRM practices. We understand care *(Ri'āya)* as providing help, attention and comfort to someone in a time of need. By compassion *(Ra'fa)* we understand a sympathetic consciousness of others. This means that a person who is concerned about the others implicitly empathizes with their situation. The focus on these informal employee-management practices allows us to go beyond a simple description of the *modus operandi* of employee management in the Middle East (Cohen, 2010). Many fundamental management values anchored in Arab countries such as KSA remain codified in informal practices (Sidani and Thornberry, 2009). Although they do not attract the interest of mainstream literature, socially responsible HRM practices exist and inspire managers to do more than simply hire, fire and pay their employees.

Our findings contribute to CSR literature by showing how and why local specificities of managerial practices cannot always be melted into one broad meaning of CSR. Practitioners may find this study helpful to thoroughly grasp the challenges which they may confront in Arab countries and the opportunities that are made available precisely by these local cultural specificities. To reach this aim, this chapter will first provide an overview of the relevant theories and key concepts of CSR available in the academic literature. Second, we will introduce the case studies of ASC in KSA and WCC in Lebanon. Subsequently, we will formulate a critical analysis of our findings and conclude by emphasizing the lessons and the implications of these case studies for the practice of CSR in the Middle East.

Internal CSR practices and employee management in medium enterprises

CSR literature usually distinguishes between internal and external social responsibilities. While the former broadly refers to social community activities and formulates general environmental concerns, the latter is understood in terms of the health and well-being of workers and their training and participation in the business. Given the intrinsic limitations of MEs, their CSR concerns are generally and mostly confined to internal matters and, naturally, HR practices play a key role. The issues at stake for MEs' HR practices that are usually discussed in CSR literature are: employees' empowerment and training, and fairness in recruitment, payment, reward and lay-off (Williamson, 2001). Moreover, the poverty of resources for MEs also accounts for the specificity of their internal CSR practices. Writing codes of conduct and/or implementing global CSR standards often requires a larger proportional investment of time, finances and energy from smaller firms than from larger organizations (Spence and Lozano, 2000). As for HR practices, Woodhams and Lupton (2006) emphasize the absence in most MEs of an HR practitioner; a fact which is obviously related to two key factors: the relatively small number of employees and the structure of ownership (both small and medium enterprises are often family owned).

Yet this does not mean that MEs recognize the importance of social responsibility less than large corporations do. The CSR policies of MEs are usually described as 'sunken CSR' (Perrini et al., 2006) or 'silent CSR' (Jenkins, 2004). Indeed, the tendency of MEs toward informality is naturally explained by the fact that this type of firm is actively managed by its owner, which makes it highly personalized (i.e. most strategic decisions are the result of the owner's personality). Within a framework where most actions are driven by personal relationships, the CSR *modus operandi* naturally tends to be informal (Russo and Tencati, 2009). When personal initiatives replace the delegation of responsibilities and codified guidelines, informal attitudes like promises and trust become fundamental. More precisely, regarding employee management, several informal practices are usually associated with CSR: ensuring the health and safety of all employees and encouraging a healthy workplace; involving employees in business decisions; considering job splitting, flexitime and other work–life balance policies; considering supporting day care for children or elderly dependents; avoiding discrimination and establishing transparent rules for hiring, salary, promotion and lay-offs (Williamson, 2001).

Addressing the question of informal CSR policy in the context of the Middle East is particularly appropriate if we take into account the proportion of small and medium enterprises (roughly 50 per cent) in the economic activity of this region (Stevenson, 2010, pp. 45–51). In contrast with other regions of the world, informal activities do not necessarily have negative connotations in the Middle East. On the contrary, in most situations they are widely accepted and are usually perceived as legitimate, advantageous and codifying Arab cultural values (Ararat, 2006; Jamali et al., 2009). An influential study (Muna, 1980) highlights the fact that the paternalistic management style is profoundly embedded in Arab values. In addition, more recent empirical research (Weir, 2000) emphasizes loyalty toward members of the same group, which includes not only immediate family but also relatives, friends and neighbors. In such a context, it is therefore not surprising to see an aversion toward systems, procedures, bureaucracy and committees (Tayeb, 2005, pp. 76–79). On another note, Islamic values aim to avoid and suppress conflicts as much as possible and to promote brotherly relationships and more broadly ethical conduct from employers and employees (Syed and Ali, 2010). Key Islamic values commonly influencing management activities include: *niyāṭ* (the fact that every act should be accompanied by intention); *itqān* (the fact of being aware in all endeavors); *iḥān* (inspiring proficiency and efficiency); *iḥlāṣ* (sincerity); *al-falāḥ* (looking for excellence); *taqwā* (continuous self-examination); *al-'adl* (piety and justice); *'amānah* (truthfulness); and *alṣabr* (patience). Further Islamic values include moderation, keeping promises, accountability, dedication, gratefulness, cleanliness, consistency and discipline (Alhabshi and Ghazali, 1994). Within the myriad of such values, and regarding the employer–employee relationship, care and compassion play a specific role and it is precisely these values that will be further emphasized (Boxes 5.1 and 5.2).

Box 5.1   Saudization/Nitaqat System

In 1994, the KSA government introduced stringent labor policies compelling private firms to employ Saudis wherever possible and to increase the number of Saudis employed by 5 per cent each year to avoid sanctions. Despite that, expatriates account for more than 95 per cent of the workforce of small and medium enterprises. The New Nitaqat system (2011) plans to divide the companies operating in KSA into three categories depending on the number of expatriates they employ: red (companies that cannot renew work permits for foreigners), yellow (companies that may not extend the work visas of their foreign employees beyond six years) and green (companies that may employ expatriates). Under the new policy, foreign workers employed by companies that do not comply with the country's Saudization quotas (categorized as 'red' and 'yellow' companies under the Nitaqat system) are free to work for companies that do comply, known as 'green' companies. The 'green' companies will be entitled to a number of benefits, such as expedited services for foreign workers' visas and the ability to transform the job categories of foreign workers into job categories reserved for Saudis.

Box 5.2   The Work and Employment of Ethnic Minorities in Lebanon

Lebanon is an Arab country of 10,452 km^2 in Western Asia. The country is a migration destination country for thousands of low-skilled Asian workers who work in domestic services. In contrast with the equal opportunities principles of the International Labour Organization, migrants in Lebanon do not always received equal chances in terms of job opportunities and career advancement. For example, the thousands of Palestinians who fled to Lebanon as refugees in 1948 are subject to Lebanese legislation that does not allow them to work. Moreover, migrants do not benefit from basic employment rights as Lebanese nationals do; unskilled workers, such as Asian domestic workers, are sometimes denied their right to a minimum wage, to work a limited number of hours a week, or even to have annual leave and join labor unions.

Source: Al Ariss (2010).

In understanding the Saudi and Lebanese organizational contexts, it is fundamental to take into account the political and economic environment. KSA is an Islamic monarchy, where the Koran is instituted as constitution and the principles of the *Shari'a* as law. Since any form of contestation is explicitly banned, no employees, whether they are Saudi nationals or immigrants, are allowed to organize unions or strikes (Atiyyah, 1999). Within this political and economic context, a key task for HR managers in KSA is to achieve a balance between employees' demands and contextual constraints. It is expected that employers should develop conciliation and arbitration skills to establish and preserve a peaceful work environment. Furthermore, KSA's recent labor policies favoring the Saudization of the workforce (Box 5.1) directly influence the entrepreneurial choice and, of course, the employer–employee relationship (Box 5.3). The competitive advantages granted by the government to Saudi nationals make it more difficult for private employers to attract skilled Saudis and even more difficult to attract enthusiastic Saudi nationals willing to dedicate their working time fully to the respective firm (Box 5.4). On the contrary, Lebanon (Box 5.2) is a multi-religious country that has witnessed periods of political instability and war. The country does not possess petroleum resources and relies heavily on the services sector. When it comes to immigrants, the HRM challenge is different for the two countries. Threatened by the prospect of seeing their work permit expire, immigrant workers are likely to accept a heavy workload combined with lower pay. So in this case, the genuine difficulty for an HR manager is to prevent the non-Saudi and non-Lebanese workers from considering that they receive unfair treatment and that they are being exploited. Such feelings of frustration are obviously considered unproductive since they are likely to hamper the workers' integration and enthusiasm (Box 5.4).

Box 5.3   Hay Group Compensation Report, 2011

This report says that: 'Saudi nationals are paid 13% higher than the general market average when we look at total cash. Pressures on organisations to achieve their target quota of Saudi nationals are apparent in the trends we see in the 2011 report which are part of a wider socio-economic story. Compared to five, or even three, years ago Saudi nationals are much more in demand and are now in the favourable position of being able to pick and choose between employers. Because organisations are obliged to comply with legislation committed to building national capability, it has become an attractive market for Saudi candidates. Saudi nationals can sell themselves a lot better and the competition for high quality Saudi talent has become more intense.'

Box 5.4 *The Economist's* **Employee Engagement Paper, 2010**

The Hay Group commissioned The Economist Intelligence Unit to carry out C-suite research which spanned Europe and the Middle East (KSA). The report says that Saudi workers show a strong work ethic yet they feel they could be more productive with greater encouragement from their employers. Employees across KSA are highly motivated. New Hay Group research shows that 91 per cent are prepared to put in extra effort for their organization. The study also shows that while most Saudi workers feel positive about their jobs and their employers, this goodwill is not necessarily translating into results. KSA has a high percentage (34) of 'frustrated' employees (i.e. people who are highly motivated but feel there are barriers to achievement). The report concludes that there is a clear opportunity here for Saudi businesses, because it shows that firms whose workers are both motivated and enabled can achieve revenue growth 4.5 times that of their peers.

To sum up, our review indicates that the mainstream approach to CSR emphasizes the homogeneity of good practices irrespective of specific contexts such as history and geography (Williams and Zinkin, 2009). Yet such a homogenous approach to CSR makes it difficult for research and management to assess and address CSR challenges that are only emerging in specific contexts (Mouawad, 2008; Safa,

2008). HRM in Saudi Arabia and Lebanon illustrates the codification of the practices and unwritten rules which govern conduct (Mellahi and Wood, 2001). Hence, contrary to the fashionable globalizing approach to CSR, the cases of ASC and WCC are helpful in explaining how informal HRM practices, such as providing care and compassion to employees (including minority ethnic immigrants), as well as personnel administration, are responsible HRM.

Practical examples of a company, country or a concept

Assad Said Corporation (ASC) in Saudi Arabia

ASC is a Saudi company established in 1977. It presently employs more than 1500 employees (see Box 5.5 for a detailed profile of ASC). We draw on interviews and observation notes in explaining the case of ASC. Interviews conducted by the second author of this paper with the company president Sheikh Mohamed Assad Ameen Said, more than 20 key managers and several unskilled employees showed that the company attaches great importance to care and compassion. The topic of care emerged in several cases.

Box 5.5   The Profile of Assad Said Corporation (ASC), KSA

ASC, a company with more than 1500 employees, including 300 managers and about 25 top managers, was established in 1977 as a subcontractor for various construction activities, mainly civil and electromechanical works. The company gradually secured its place as a major contractor for complete civil and architectural works on various civil buildings, power plants, substations, desalination plants, strategic fences, TV, radio and transmitter stations and overhead transmission lines with major contractors such as Siemens, General Electric Co., NEI/Reyrolle, SST, Hyundai, ABB, ALSTOM, BechTel and Mitsui, to name but a few. The company is presided over and managed by its founder, Sheikh Mohammad Assad Ameen Said, and has gained an excellent reputation for the quality and punctual delivery of all its works.

The case of Raju (pseudonym) illustrates such concern. Raju (Indian, 55 years old) is a project manager at ASC. He has been working for the company for more than 10 years. Raju has left ASC twice for another employer, searching for better career opportunities. However, he always ended up returning to work at ASC. While he complained that salaries are relatively better in multinational companies compared with what he earns at ASC, he reported not being able to find the same care and compassion that was available for him at ASC. For instance, the president gave him financial assistance to get married and listened to his professional and personal problems as well as trying to provide solutions and support whenever possible. Raju described ASC as more like a family where he found job security and personal and professional comfort. Other interviews with less-skilled employees showed similar trends. For instance, Karthik (Indian, 45 years old) reported that while in some Saudi companies minority ethnic migrants might be discriminated against, the president of ASC was characterized by honesty and humbleness. Again, he helped Karthik to establish himself in the country, provided care at both a professional and a personal level, and trusted him by giving him autonomy in his work. Karthik mentioned being a committed employee. He has been working at ASC since the very early days of the company.

One imagines that a president of a 1500-employee company might be unapproachable. On the contrary, interviews and observation notes showed that this was not the case at ASC. Such patterns were noticeable in three ways. First, all of the interviewed participants mentioned having access to the president via mobile phone and being able to reach him easily, at almost any time. Second, at prayer times, the president took the time to perform prayers with all practicing Muslim employees. Before and after each prayer time, a room was provided for the employees to discuss any issues with the president and share their concerns. If needed, they were invited to join him in his main office to discuss the matter further. Here it is important to mention that all interviewees (Muslims and non-Muslims) mentioned having freedom of religion at ASC. Third, interviewees mentioned that it was possible for them to meet with the president in his office without the need for an appointment. Observation showed that employees from all levels popped up to the president's office to share their concerns, without always giving prior notice.

Interviews conducted with ASC's president demonstrated his worldview that every employee is of great importance to the success of the company's projects. For example, the president encourages his employees by giving them financial and non-financial incentives. Rather than focusing on making financial benefits, the president expressed the key importance of paying his employees their salaries in a timely fashion, keeping them committed to ASC, securing their career development, and providing them with care at the professional and personal levels. Here an example can be mentioned. While training was not yet institutionalized as a human resource development strategy at ASC, the president organizes frequent training sessions for his managers and employees. At the time of the interviews, all ASC project managers were attending a series of training sessions on the topic of project management. Those who successfully completed the training were given certificates signed personally by the president. Group interviews were conducted with these same employees; the aim being to understand the way that they perceived these training sessions. All of the interviewees reported having a feeling of being valued as they were offered possibilities to develop their professional competencies. Several employees mentioned that such training provided them with career development opportunities. Another topic that emerged from these interviews was the importance of honesty in employment relations. The president repeated several times that honest relations with the clients and employees ensures that ASC remains a well-reputed company. In the same way, employees are expected to uphold a high level of honesty and ethical conduct.

Window Cleaning Company (WCC) in Lebanon

WCC (Box 5.6) has 453 professionally trained staff, most of them without university or even school qualifications. Most of the employees are non-Lebanese and come from India, Bangladesh, Syria, Iraq and Egypt, and almost 30 per cent of them are women. Teams are led by several key managers who contribute to the success of HRM at WCC. The company ensures that its employees are trained to achieve professional excellence in the cleaning sector. This is important as it is reflected in higher levels of client satisfaction. In the same way, the company values the safety and health of its employees and has therefore adopted guidelines and created conditions that enable its staff to exercise their activities securely.

Box 5.6   The Profile of Window Cleaning Company (WCC), Lebanon

Window Cleaning Company (WCC) is a Lebanese enterprise, based in Beirut, which is owned and managed by the Lebanese-Canadian couple Joe and Rosi Bachaalani. The company specializes in the professional cleaning business. Since it was founded in 1997, the company has witnessed tremendous growth in Lebanon and gained clients in several business sectors, including more than 188 high-rise towers, hotels, residential buildings and banks, among others. The company specializes in aluminium frames and rubber-gasket repairs using high-quality German and US cleaning products.

Based on an interview with owner/manager Joe Bachaalani, as well as on-field observations, we will expand on two relevant issues in terms of informal, caring HRM at WCC. Like many other MEs in Lebanon, WCC does not have an HR manager. Instead, Joe is the one who manages HR matters. In terms of informal supportive HR practices, we will discuss two examples: employee recognition and career development at WCC.

The company adopts a philosophy where business should not only be profitable but also be enjoyable. With this in mind, the 'Employee of the month' award was designed to recognize employees' efforts in making WCC more productive. In this way, every month, Joe and his management team choose an employee who has demonstrated excellent performance. This could be in terms of satisfying a client, successfully completing their professional training or enhancing team cohesion, for example. When the award is given, Joe organizes a team meeting where a large photo of the employee is hooked on the wall of the company's main entrance to provide a lighter atmosphere and in recognition of the employee's professional efforts. Furthermore, a bonus sum of money is awarded to this same employee. During this monthly event, employees celebrate their success and discuss and share their experiences. Also, this has proven to be an excellent opportunity to show that Joe cares about them and that he recognizes their work.

The career development of employees at WCC is organized in two key stages: first, providing adequate training for new employees to prepare them for undertaking technical work; and second, identifying and accompanying employees who demonstrate leadership skills in order to place them in managerial positions. We will discuss these two issues in this same order. First, training: due to a shortage of skilled workers, most of the immigrant employees are selected to work at WCC when they are still in their country of origin. Usually, they are referred by other WCC employees. Many of them come without any prior experience in the cleaning sector. In addition, for non-Arabic speakers, there is the additional language barrier when moving to work in Lebanon. To overcome these challenges, Joe has established professional training modules, which last 4–5 days, designed in the native language of the employees and delivered by experienced staff. The trainers usually share the cultural background of the new employees and use a wide range of training techniques such as videos, practical cases and group fieldwork participation. These techniques have proved to be extremely effective in enhancing the technical skills of the employees and in accommodating them in terms of linguistic needs. Second, career development: employees are hired with five-year contracts that can be renewed and a starting salary of US$350 a month for a cleaner. However, Joe's approach is to promote those who prove to have leadership skills to supervisory positions. In this way, after only a few years, an employee can take a supervisory position with a salary of US$600–800 and take advantage of the free tickets offered to them once every two years by WCC to visit their country of origin. This is usually associated with an increase in their annual leave and team management responsibilities. This career development technique has proved to be a main contributing factor in keeping employees within the company, and employees remain, on average, for a seven-year period.

Discussion

Our study clearly indicates the implicit awareness of an employer's social responsibility in employee management. Neither the employer nor the employees at ASC, or even WCC, used the following words (which are currently fashionable in contemporary academia): stakeholder, responsible management and leadership practices, equal opportunities, diversity management, glass-ceiling, accountable governance and human resource management. Despite the lack of a mainstream CSR vocabulary, we note several key concepts that are helpful for disclosing and emphasizing several managerial practices that are akin to social responsibility in employee management. During the interviews conducted at ASC and WCC, the ideas of 'compassion' and 'care' were mentioned frequently, by both the employer and the employees. These concepts refer to informal managerial approaches that positively influence employee management (Mellahi and Wood, 2001). Several practices confirmed this observation. For instance, when the employer at ASC anticipated the monthly payment of some worse-off employees in order to satisfy their urgent needs or when the president of WCC paid attention to the specific training needs of his foreign workers, they obviously demonstrated an acute sense of responsibility, which is fully compatible with current practices in CSR. Although these attitudes toward employees are not codified, they are nonetheless akin to CSR.

While the position of HR manager existed at ASC, his title was 'personnel manager' and his work was limited to administrative issues, such as securing papers for migrant workers. Nevertheless, WCC did not have an HR manager. The cases of ASC and WCC show that the role of an HR manager in a large Western corporation is played in the Middle East by the owner himself. This specificity, relative to MEs, is amplified by the social and cultural contexts of KSA and Lebanon. Here, the values are embedded in a long-lasting paternalistic tradition. In light of this particular fact, the employer–employee relationship would seem to be established on a one-to-one basis, rather than as part of a more complex managerial process. One interesting outcome of this paternalistic strategy is that, in the case of ASC and WCC, the success of the practices akin to social responsibility depends entirely on the employer himself. This observation is to be compared and contrasted with other findings regarding Western MEs, where the success of CSR implementation depends essentially on the employees' motivation and enthusiasm (Collier and Esteban, 2007). In Western contexts, the main burden of successfully implementing social responsibility in the daily life of the company is borne by employees. However, returning to ASC and WCC, the fact that a firm's CSR policy depends on one person rather than on procedures and policies is not necessarily problematic. Such personal relationships, with the employer and the employees taking on CSR in an informal manner, have had a positive impact on employee achievement at ASC and WCC. Evidence of this outcome was our participants' perception of having professional satisfaction, feelings of comfort at a personal level, a high commitment to the company and a good relationship with its hierarchy.

In principle, it would seem more difficult for the owner of a medium (and even more so of a small) enterprise to 'window dress'. Very often, the various non-governmental organizations that monitor large corporations release reports regarding fake or hypocritical CSR statements. Hence, the respective corporations are blamed for using CSR as a communication tool or as a label to increase their profits without doing anything concrete in the field of social responsibility. Clearly, given the specific context in which ASC operates, a window-dressing operation becomes much more difficult. This is especially the case because the employer–employee relationship described at ASC exists mainly on a one-to-one basis. Within this type of relationship, fuzzy promises, lies and failures to respect verbal agreements are easily detected and sanctioned by the employees (Dessler and Al Ariss, 2012). For instance, lying to skilful Saudi workers may have severe consequences in the short term for the firm because these workers can quickly find another job. When it comes to the context of Lebanon, WCC owners also recognize that failing to live up to employees' expectations would quickly result in an increased staff turnover which would automatically decrease productivity and engender the loss of the initial investment in employee training.

Our field study indicated that trust is intimately linked to care and compassion. This virtuous circle is considered a key CSR practice in employee management (Andersson et al., 2007). One of the employer's strategies in becoming trustworthy is to assist his employees with their everyday difficulties. So, the owners of ASC and WCC shared with us their endeavors to make themselves available so that their employees have the feeling that they can rely upon them. At ASC, the offer of assistance for specific events like weddings or urgent financial difficulties establishes an intimate link between employer and employee. The same is applicable at WCC in terms of attending to employees' needs in terms of training and career development. In both cases the migrant workers pose specific challenges; ASC needs to sponsor their work permit (according to labor laws in

KSA), while WCC has to mobilize important resources for their integration. Positive past experiences are often perceived by employees as a sign that the employer is trustworthy. They diffuse an image of the character and the personality of the employer among workers. It is based on precisely this image that employees are inclined to trust the employer and, therefore, accept a heavy workload or lower pay during periods of economic downturn.

In the cases of ASC and WCC we found that care and compassion were embedded in Arabic culture. While in Western corporate cultures the focus is on employees' well-being (Al Ariss, 2011), in the Arab cultural context, a person who cares empathizes with someone else by establishing an organic and familiar link with him. Such an attitude goes beyond mere charity and assistance and endeavors to establish close employee–employer bonds. Hence, it is particularly interesting to observe that the employer–employee relationship at ASC extends to after-work time and to the employee's family as well. Such a permeable interpretation of the private sphere is profoundly anchored in Arab values and differs radically from the classical Western view (Habermas, 1989). In Western cultures, the permeability of the private sphere is morally unacceptable because it is perceived as a violation of the right to privacy (Parent, 1983). Conversely, during our interviews conducted at ASC we noted that within the Arab context, the employer–employee exchange of mobile-phone numbers is perceived by most employees as a sign of proximity with their employer and not at all as a possible intrusion into their private lives. This might suggest that the paternalistic framework predominant in Arab companies, and especially in KSA, transforms the firm into a family (Mellahi and Wood, 2001).

In this example, proximity engenders a virtuous circle of mutual caring. The interviewees, both employers and employees, supported the statement that the reciprocity between employee and employer strengthens their professional rapport and sets the ground for a trustworthy association. These findings contrast sharply with the worries of Janjuha-Jivraj (2004), which state that reciprocity and informal CSR frameworks might create conditions for dissatisfaction and exploitative behavior. Furthermore, the interviews conducted at WCC allowed us to understand that informal CSR practices are not necessarily sporadic nor randomly applied (Spence and Painter-Morland, 2010). On the contrary, interpersonal relationships on a one-to-one basis, guided by key values such as care and compassion, tend to be constant and long-lasting. The stability of these practices is, for instance, reflected at WCC in the monthly award for the best employee. In this case, the employees' confidence can be gained only if the choice of best employee is transparent and based on stable criteria.

A final idea that should be emphasized from these interviews is the explicit awareness of the employer that responsible managerial practices are capable of bringing important economic value. During the interviews, the presidents' managerial styles suggested that they perceive the improvement in the quality of life of their workforce – and, more generally, the employees' well-being – as essential for the competitiveness of their business. Indeed, the fact that some employees have returned to ASC after less-satisfying experiences elsewhere is perceived by the employer as proof of the success of his employee management strategy, which is akin to social responsibility. Alternatively, the comparatively low rate of staff turnover encourages the owner of WCC to pursue his employee management strategy based on care and compassion. Training and development for employees are activities that may support the future success of the business and ensure the workers' continued employability.

Conclusions and implications

The informal CSR strategies illustrated here are examples of a learning-by-doing type of entrepreneurial expertise (Salerno, 2008). Given the specificity of the economic context of the Saudization policies in KSA (Box 5.1), the entrepreneurs and managers, especially those working for MEs, need to develop new strategies for attracting a qualified and motivated workforce (Box 5.3). CSR can represent a genuine competitive advantage for employees and employers. As explained above, one of the factors of success in attracting and retaining skilled and motivated employees is the fair treatment they receive. Indeed, at ASC, the president considers that his own responsibility toward employers goes beyond mere legal obligation. In giving all his employees a fair and equal chance to seek, develop and maximize their potential he recognizes a concrete opportunity to achieve a loyal and trustworthy employer–employee relationship. The case of WCC clearly shows us the importance of a coherent employee management strategy. To seize the returns for the initial investment in training, employers must commit to high standards of social responsibility. Furthermore, this commitment must be constant through time.

Grounded in Arab values, attitudes such as care and compassion can introduce a virtuous circle of trust in the workplace. Given this objective, there is no particular need to reiterate or imitate Western CSR practices. Employer–employee relationships developed on a one-to-one basis appear to be very beneficial from several points of view. First, an informal CSR strategy is coherent because once employees relate because of a personal promise, it becomes morally unacceptable for the employer to discontinue this strategy. Second, the employer gains the loyalty of the workforce; therefore, employees become more reluctant to leave the firm and work with more enthusiasm. Third, worse-off employees and those who would usually feel discriminated against gain the reassurance of a fair workplace.

Summary and recommendations

A central assumption in mainstream CSR is that ethical principles are applicable worldwide, as the recent development of ISO 26000 illustrates. Drawing on a literature review and the case studies of ASC in KSA and WCC in Lebanon, we demonstrate that this global approach to CSR veils context-specific and informal HRM practices that are socially responsible. Care and compassion are examples of key, but overlooked, components. Burgeoning management studies in Arab countries (Rettab et al., 2009) show that CSR has a positive relationship with organizational performance – financial performance, employee commitment and corporate reputation. Our study extends such research by showing that informal CSR practices, such as care and compassion, lead to responsible HRM. This increases employees' commitment to the company and enthusiasm in the workplace and has implications at the individual, organizational and policy-making levels. At the individual level, we find that even in political contexts shaped by strict policies on migrants' employment (Box 5.1), there are friendly workplaces, like ASC, that support socially responsible management.

At the organizational level, informal practices of socially responsible management are important. As is shown by the cases of ASC and WCC, these practices can provide a genuine comparative advantage to an employer in the competition for skilled employees. In addition, these practices may contribute toward alleviating the feelings of injustice that immigrant workers are likely to experience (especially when employment policies are strict, as is the case within the government Nitaqat system—see Box 5.1), and more generally, to enhancing the motivation of all workers. Informal CSR practices based on care and compassion may be ordered, transparent and long-lasting given the family like structure of the firm. Companies can extend such approaches and translate their informal care and compassion practices to formal ethical guidelines. This additional step in CSR would be especially necessary when MEs expand their activities and increase the number of their employees. Indeed, care and compassion are very demanding activities and their success depends on the number of people who need them. So, at the time when a responsible employer understands that it is no longer possible to personalize relationships on a one-to-one basis, the need for a switch to a more formal CSR strategy would arise. Of course, even in the case of large corporations, the written ethical codes of conducts and other formal CSR strategies may be complemented by occasional informal practices in a satisfactory manner.

At the policy making level, more is needed in terms of supporting migrant workers, who constitute a large share of the Arab labor markets. Without such support, companies need to play the role of institutional structures in providing care to their employees. For instance, in terms of HR development, governments in countries like KSA and Lebanon can issue policies and guidelines to encourage companies to adopt socially responsible practices. These might include fostering ethical conduct and anti-discrimination actions, providing training for employees and securing career development for migrants, regardless of their ethnic origin.

References

Abbas, J. A. (2010) 'Islamic Challenges to HR in Modern Organizations', *Personnel Review*, vol. 39, no. 6, pp. 692–711.

Al Ariss, A. (2010) 'Religious Diversity in Lebanon: Lessons from a Small Country to the Global World'. In M. Özbilgin and J. Syed (eds), *Managing Cultural Diversity in Asia: A Research Companion* (New York: Edward Elgar Publishing), pp. 56–72.

Al Ariss, A. (2012) 'Human Resource Management', *Academy of Management Learning and Education*, vol. 11, no. 1, pp. 147–151.

Alhabshi, S. O. and Ghazali, A. H. (1994) *Islamic Values and Management* (Kuala Lumpur: Institute of Islamic Understanding Malaysia (IKIM)).

Andersson, L. M., Giacalone, R. A., and Jurkiewicz, C. L. (2007) 'On the Relationship of Hope and Gratitude to Corporate Social Responsiblity', *Journal of Business Ethics*, vol. 70, pp. 401–409.

Ararat, M. (2006) 'Corporate Social Responsibility Across Middle East and North Africa', *World Bank Working Paper*.

Atiyyah, H. S. (1999) 'Public Organisations' Effectiveness and its Determinants in a Developing Country', *Cross Cultural Management*, vol. 6, no. 2, pp. 8–21.

Bozionelos, N. (2009) 'Expatriation Outside the Boundaries of the Multinational Corporation: a Study with Expatriate Nurses in Saudi Arabia', *Human Resource Management*, vol. 48, no. 1, pp. 111–134.

Cohen, E. (2010) *CSR for HR: A Necessary Partnership for Advancing Responsible Business* (Practices Sheffield: Greenleaf Publishing).

Collier, J. and Esteban, R. (2007) 'Corporate Social Responsibility and Employee Commitment', *Business Ethics: A European Review*, vol. 16, no. 1, pp. 19–33.

Dessler, G. and Al Ariss, A. (2012) *Human Resource Management*, Arab World ed. (London: Pearson).

Habermas, J. (1989) *The Structural Transformation of the Public Sphere: An Inquiry into a Category of Bourgeois Society, Studies in Contemporary German Social Thought* (Cambridge, MA: MIT Press).

Jamali, D. and Abdallah, H. (2009) 'Diversity Management Rhetoric Vs Reality: Insights from the Lebanese Context'. In M. Özbilgin and J. Syed (eds), *Diversity Management in Asia: A Research Companion* (Cheltenham and New York: Edward Elgar).

Jamali, D., Safieddine, A., and Daouk, M. (2006) 'The Glass Ceiling: Some Positive Trends from the Lebanese Banking Sector', *Women in Management Review*, vol. 21, no. 8, pp. 625–642.

Jamali, D., Sidani, Y., and El-Asmar, K. (2009) 'Changing Managerial CSR Orientations: A Three Country. Comparative Analysis of Lebanon, Syria and Jordan', *Journal of Business Ethics*, vol. 85, pp. 173–192.

Janjuha-Jivraj, S. (2004) 'The Sustainability of Informal Ethnic Business Networks'. In L. Spence (ed.), *The Social World of Small and Medium Sized Enterprises: Social Capital and Responsibility* (London: Palgrave Macmillan).

Jenkins, H. (2004) 'A Critique of Conventional CSR Theory: An SME Perspective', *Journal of General Management*, vol. 29, no. 4, pp. 37–57.

Mellahi, K. and Wood, G. T. (2001) 'Human Resource Management in Saudi Arabia' In Research in Employment Relations, *Human Resource Management in Developing Countries* (London: Routledge), pp. 135–153.

Moran, R. T., Harris, Ph. R., and Moran, S. V. (2007) *Managing Cultural Differences: Global Leadership Strategies for the 21st Century* (Oxford: Butterworth-Heinemann).

Mouawad, N. (2008) 'The Need for Effective CSR in the Middle East', *Executive*, vol. 110, September, pp. 100–101.

Muna, F. A. (1980) *The Arab Executive* (London: Macmillan).

Parent, W. (1983) 'Privacy, Morality and the Law', *Philosophy and Public Affairs*, vol. 12, pp. 269–288.

Perrini, F., Pogutz S., and Tencati, A. (2006) 'Corporate Social Responsibility in Italy: State of the Art', *Journal of Business Strategies*, vol. 23, no. 1, pp. 65–91.

Rettab, B., Brik, A. B., and Mellahi, K. (2009) 'A Study of Management Perceptions of the Impact of Corporate Social Responsibility on Organisational Performance in Emerging Economies: The Case of Dubai', *Journal of Business Ethics*, vol. 89, no. 3, pp. 371–390.

Russo, A. and Tencati, A. (2009) 'Formal vs. Informal CSR Strategies: Evidence from Italian Micro, Small, Medium-Sized, and Large Firms', *Journal of Business Ethics*, vol. 85, no. 2, pp. 339–353.

Safa, O. (2008) 'The Challenge CSR Faces in The MENA Region', *Executive*, vol. 110, September, p. 96.

Salerno, J. (2008) 'The Entrepreneur: Real and Imagined', *Quarterly Journal of Austrian Economics*, vol. 8, no. 4, pp. 188–207.

Sidani, Y. M. and Jamali, D. (2010) 'The Egyptian Worker: Work Beliefs and Attitudes', *Journal of Business Ethics*, vol. 92, no. 3, pp. 433–450.

Sidani, Y. M. and Thornberry, J. (2009) 'The Current Arab Work Ethic: Antecedents, Implications, and Potential Remedies', *Journal of Business Ethics*, vol. 91, no. 1, pp. 35–49.

Spence, L. J. (1999) 'Does Size Matter? The State of the Art in Small Business Ethics', *Business Ethics. A European Review*, vol. 8, no. 3, pp. 163–174.

Spence, L. J. and Lozano J. F. (2000) 'Communicating About Ethics with Small Firms. Experiences from the U.K. And Spain', *Journal of Business Ethics*, vol. 27, no. 1, pp. 43–53.

Spence, L. J. and Painter-Morland, M. (2010) *Ethics in Small and Medium Sized Enterprises* (Dordrecht: Springer).

Stevenson, L. (2010) *Private Sector and Enterprise Development: Fostering Growth in the Middle East and North Africa* (Cheltenham: Edward Elgar).

Syed, J. and Ali, A. J. (2010) 'Principles of Employment Relations in Islam: A Normative View', *Employee Relations*, vol. 32, no. 5, pp. 454–469.

Tayeb, M. H. (2005) *International Human Resource Management: A Multinational Company Perspective* (Oxford: Oxford University Press).

Tilley, F. (2000) 'Small Firm Environmental Ethics: How Deep Do They Go?', *Business Ethics: A European Review*, vol. 9, no. 1, pp. 31–41.

Weir, D. (2000) 'Management in the Arab Middle East'. In M. H. Tayeb (ed.), *International Business: Theories, Policies and Practices* (London: Pearson Education), pp. 501–517.

Williams, G. and Zinkin, J. (2009) 'Islam and CSR: A Study of the Compatibility Between the Tenets of Islam and the UN Global Compact', *Journal of Business Ethics*, vol. 91, no. 4, pp. 519–533.

Williamson, I. O. (2001) 'Employer Legitimacy and Recruitment Success in Small Businesses', *Entrepreneurship, Theory and Practice*, vol. 24, no. 1, p. 27.

Woodhams, C. and Lupton, B. (2006) 'Does Size Matter? Gender-Based Equal Opportunity in UK Small and Medium Enterprises', *Women in Management Review*, vol. 21, no. 2, pp. 143–169.

6

Corporate Environmental Responsibility in Jordan: The Potential and Limits

Muna Y. Hindiyeh, Malyuba Abu-Daabes and Haitham E. Salti

Introduction

The world is facing unique environmental challenges. There is a record loss of biodiversity and long-term damage to ecosystems; pollution of the atmosphere and the consequences of climate change; waste production and disposal; natural resource depletion; the impact of using chemicals and toxic substance disposal; damaged aquatic ecosystems and land degradation. There is a need to identify the options to reduce and eliminate unsustainable volumes and patterns of production and consumption to ensure that the resource consumption per person becomes sustainable.

The business sector is considered to be one of the biggest culprits of environmental degradation. Industry mines, extracts, shovels, burns, wastes and pumps, abusing the web of life. The living system and the life support systems of Earth are consequently in decline and the biosphere that supports human beings is corrupted. Governmental policies have failed to control such practices, as well as the private sector primarily focusing on profits. While governments may introduce laws that protect the environment and the current and future economic and social needs and rights of its citizens, many businesses recognize a commercial advantage in going beyond what is required by law.

Companies are expected to take an active role, and to initiate the addressing of social and environmental activities. These activities and issues that relate to corporate social responsibility (CSR) may include employment, health and safety, training and education, poverty, women's issues, safe products and adopting environmentally friendly technology (ISO, 2010). Furthermore, environmental responsibility is a precondition for the survival and prosperity of humankind. Environmental education and capacity building is fundamental in promoting the development of sustainable societies and lifestyles.

Tapping the resources and goodwill of corporations is essential, especially in countries like Jordan where privatization and liberalization are strongly being pursued by the government and where a new role for the private sector is envisioned. In addition to donating financial resources to ongoing sustainable development efforts, the private sector can also exercise CSR by investing in a sound environment in which to do business, as well as managing the direct costs and risks of conducting this business (United Nations Development Programme (UNDP), 2003).

This chapter will focus on an assessment of corporate environmental responsibility (CER) in Jordanian private-sector enterprises with respect to the three United Nations (UN) Global Compact (GC) principles: 7, 8 and 9. We will show how Jordanian companies regard GC, CSR, CER, environmentally friendly technology and clean production (CP) programs. In addition, the current national-level initiatives and the adoption of environmentally friendly technology and practices, including policy levels, legislation, implementation and monitoring, will be discussed. This chapter will also include a qualitative discussion on the market drivers and CER language in the Jordanian context from the cultural, religious, academic and business literature.

A case study will focus on CER in the pharmaceutical sector in Jordan. Investigations will analyze the environmental performance of two representative case companies, tackling the gaps and employing a CP approach to provide cost-effective alternatives for protecting the environment in Jordan.

Literature review

The essential characteristic of social responsibility is the willingness of an organization to incorporate social and environmental considerations in its decision-making and be accountable for the impact of its decisions and activities on society and the environment, through transparent and ethical behavior that contributes to sustainable development (ISO 26000, 2010). The International Standard Organisation's ISO 26000 standard provides guidance on the underlying principles of social responsibility – recognizing social responsibility and engaging stakeholders, the core subjects and issues pertaining to social responsibility, and ways to integrate socially responsible behavior into an organization. It also emphasizes the importance of results and improvements in performance on social responsibility (ISO 26000, 2010).

The decisions and activities of organizations invariably have an impact on the environment no matter where the organizations are located. These impacts may be associated with the organization's use of resources, the location of the activities of the organization, the generation of pollution and wastes, and the impact of the organization's activities on natural habitats. To reduce their environmental impact, organizations should adopt an integrated approach that takes into consideration the direct and indirect economic, social, health and environmental implications of their decisions and activities (ISO 26000, 2010). Relevant technical tools, such as standards from the ISO 14000 series of standards, can be used as an overall framework to assist an organization in addressing environmental issues in a systematic manner. These tools should then be considered when evaluating environmental performance, in quantifying and reporting greenhouse gas emissions, in life-cycle assessment, design for the environment, environmental labeling and environmental communication.

Companies which practice CER have experienced a range of benefits, such as improved financial performance, reduced operating costs, enhanced brand image and reputation, increased sales and customer loyalty, better productivity and quality, increased ability to attract and retain employees, reduced regulatory oversight and access to capital (Hohnen, 2007; UN Global Compact, 2007).

The World Business Council for Sustainable Development (WBCSD) has produced a matrix of key CSR issues, with appropriate indicators from stakeholder groups, for companies developing their own set of criteria or indicators to correspond to their social footprint (Table 6.1). The identified key CSR issues that were

Table 6.1 Matrix of Key CSR Issues with Appropriate Indicators by Stakeholders

Stakeholders key issue	Company owners, shareholders and investors	Employees	Customers	Business partners
Impact on environment	▲ Disaster planning/ risk assessment; ▲ incidence of disasters/near misses; ▲ % of employees trained.	▲ Resource consumption quantity of resource saved through employee action.	▲ Customer awareness about product use/disposal; ▲ trends in customer behavior.	▲ Environmental standards; ▲ % of partners with external certification of 'Environment Management System' recognized against independent standard.

Stakeholders key issue	Suppliers	Competitors	Government regulators	NGOs, pressure groups, influencers, communities
Impact on environment	▲ Promoting high standards in suppliers; ▲ % of suppliers achieving environmental standard.	▲ Commercial exploitation; ▲ market share; ▲ monopoly investigations complaints.	▲ Meeting standards; ▲ third-party ratings and awards.	▲ Effectiveness of use of expertise; ▲ stakeholder perception; ▲ investment in environmental research; ▲ impact on local environment, air pollution.

Source: WBCSD (2000). Corporate Social Responsibility: Making good business sense.

put in the vertical axis include: values and governance, regulation and controls, business operations, accountability and disclosure, human rights, employee rights/working conditions, business context, social impact/investment, impact on other species and on environment. The horizontal axis identifies the stakeholder groups, including company owners/stakeholders/investors, employees, customers, business partners, suppliers, competitors, government regulators, non-governmental organizations (NGOs)/pressure groups/influences and communities. Putting the various pieces together, the matrix illustrates how indicators can reflect CSR practice (WBCSD, 2000). For example, under the key issue of impact on the environment, suggested indicators for the employees' stakeholder group concern resource consumption and the quantity of resource saved through employee action; for the suppliers' stakeholder group, the suggestions relate to promoting high standards for suppliers and the percentage of suppliers achieving environmental standards.

In an attempt to establish a common ground for private enterprises implementing CSR, the GC has developed ten principles covering the areas of human rights, labor, the environment and anti-corruption. These principles enjoy universal consensus as they are derived from The Universal Declaration of Human Rights (1948), The International Labor Organization's Declaration on Fundamental Principles and Rights at Work (1998) and The Rio Declaration on Environment and Development (1992).

The UN Global Compact (2007) aims to increase the role of the private sector and civil society organizations in collectively addressing issues related to CSR. It enables the private sector in Jordan to benefit from an international framework that ensures responsible business practices through the integration of the ten GC principles into companies' strategies and operations, and it also promotes greater involvement of the private sector in development.

The environment covers three principles within the GC initiatives. The first is 'Principle 7' which, strengthening the key element of a precautionary approach, from a business perspective, is the idea of prevention rather than cure. In other words, it is more cost-effective to take early action to ensure that irreversible environmental damage does not occur. On the other hand, 'Principle 8' emphasizes a business gaining its legitimacy through meeting the needs of society, and increasingly society is expressing a clear need for more environmentally sustainable practices. One way for business to demonstrate its commitment to greater environmental responsibility is by changing its modus operandi from the so-called 'traditional methods' to more responsible approaches to addressing environmental issues.

The third, 'Principle 9', focuses on environmentally proficient technologies, and allows us to reduce the use of finite resources and encourages us to use existing resources more efficiently. For example, an improvement in the power-to-weight ratio of batteries has led to a significant reduction in the use of toxic heavy metals while bringing substantial benefits to the consumer. Waste storage, treatment and disposal are costly in financial as well as environmental and social terms.

Since environmentally sound technologies generate less waste and residue, the continued use of inefficient technologies can represent increased operating costs for business. In addition, it results in a retrospective focus on control and remediation rather than prevention. On the other hand, avoiding environmental impacts through pollution prevention and ecological product design increases the efficiency and overall competitiveness of the company and may also lead to new business opportunities. As environmentally sound technologies reduce operating inefficiencies, they also lead to lower emissions of environmental contaminants.

Manufacturing goods and providing services uses resources and generates waste. These are costs to business that can be significantly reduced by (EPA, 2000):

- improved management of materials, processes and operations;
- waste minimization, including waste avoidance, reuse and recycling;
- careful design and selection of products and services; and
- optimization of processes, operations and resource usage through appropriate choice of technologies and design.

In the past, regulatory control and legal requirements were the forces compelling organizations to minimize pollution and waste. Today, due to the ever-increasing costs of waste management and the business imperative to minimize operating costs through efficiency, CP has become a necessity rather than an option.

CP and the triple bottom line (EPA, 2000)

Financial

CP improves a company's financial bottom line by:

- increasing efficiency and productivity;
- reducing costs for waste disposal and treatment;
- reducing raw material, energy and water costs;
- reducing liability risks.

Environmental

CP improves a company's environmental bottom line by:

- reducing pollution of waterways, air and land; and
- reducing risk of non-compliance with regulatory requirements.

Social

CP improves a company's social bottom line by:

- enhancing corporate profile and marketing edge by demonstrating environmental responsibility (which also indirectly improves its financial bottom line);
- reducing health and safety risks; and
- improving staff morale and service.

The UN Environment Program (UNEP) defines CP as 'the continuous application of an integrated preventive environmental strategy applied to processes, products and services to increase overall efficiency and reduce risks to humans and the environment.' CP is an extensive, general term that focuses on all prospects of inputs, production and outputs. It certainly addresses attitudes and management philosophy as well as business practices. It is not a question of changing equipment; it is a matter of changing attitudes and behavior in doing business (Burton Hamner, 1996).

CER in the Jordanian context

The political system in Jordan encourages civil society organizations to play an important role in the social and economic arena (Brand, 1998). The Jordanian culture is mainly based on Arabic and

Islamic customary laws, which call for assisting the needy, non-discrimination, equal opportunities, accountability, to fight against corruption and to respect human rights and the environment. Jordanian culture is considered as one of the driving forces behind CSR activities within Jordanian companies (Elian, 2005). The private sector in Jordan has a long history of philanthropy, practiced mainly in the form of active efforts to promote human welfare.

The latest statistical figures and economic indicators have shown that Jordan is still facing increasing poverty and unemployment levels, up to 13.3 and 12.7 per cent, respectively (Department of Statistics of Jordan, 2008). Moreover, the latest increase in fuel prices has triggered another hike in prices that has led to a decline in living standards and the purchasing power of the local currency (Jordanian Dinar (JD)). Such an increase might make poverty more severe, particularly for those with a low income. Because the Jordanian government alone cannot solve the country's economic difficulties, there is an urgent need for local companies to do more in the area of CSR and to work hand-in-hand with other institutions and establishments of the public and private sectors for the sake of the well-being of society (Emerging Jordan & American Chamber of Commerce, 2005).

Over the past 28 years, Jordan has taken action to protect its natural resources after it realized that environmental pollution was impeding the country's development and reducing its progress opportunities. This action took the form of establishing institutions, developing laws, regulations, strategies and action plans and ratifying international conventions. Since 2006, to be able to lead a sustainable life, Jordan has introduced programs and incorporated actions in some of its institutions to introduce cleaner production technologies and eco-efficiency techniques. Jordan Clean Production Program (JCPP) is one of the programs that has been introduced recently. It aims to develop and update environmental policy, raising awareness and providing technical assistance. JCPP follows the international and European standards that respond to the main environmental challenges caused by its industry.

The Jordanian Network for Environmentally Friendly Industries (JNEFI) was launched in 1999, while in 2002 a CP program funded by the Swiss government started helping Jordanian industries to implement environmentally friendly technologies.

In Jordan, the focus on CSR started in 2005, with increasing emphasis in 2007, particularly in the media, conferences and forums with strong political patronage and support. King Abdullah II's Award for Excellence is the highest level of quality recognition in Jordan. It is aimed at enhancing the competitiveness of Jordanian businesses by promoting quality awareness and performance excellence, recognizing the quality and business achievements of Jordanian organizations. The award publicizes the successful performance strategies of these organizations, promotes and shares them. In 2006, CSR was included and recognized as an important criterion for the award.

Since 2006, the Cleaner Production Excellence Model Award (CP Excellence) has been implemented as an incentive tool that guarantees international recognition for companies in Jordan, thus enabling them access to national and international markets in a competitive and sustainable manner. The CP Excellence aims at helping the implementation and improvement of a comprehensive CP system across industrial facilities. It focuses on the three pillars of sustainable development: environmental aspects, social issues and economic efficiency.

Having signed trade agreements with the European Union, the USA and the Arab region, Jordan has opened up new market opportunities. Environment protection and management is a precondition for industry to access those markets. Moreover, consideration of the environmental dimension has become more than just a legal constraint; it is also a financial imperative if companies wish to remain in the world market.

The main hot spots and areas of special concern for environmental pollution in Jordan are caused by the emission of several industries scattered all over the country as they are shown in Table 6.2.

The Government of Jordan has entered into a number of regional and international conventions, protocols and agreements related to environmental protection. Some of these are directly related to cleaner production and pollution prevention, such as:

- International Rotterdam Convention, signed and ratified July 2002.
- Montreal Protocol on Substances that Deplete the Ozone Layer, ratified 1995.

- Kyoto Protocol on Climate Change, signed January 17, 2003 and ratified February 16, 2005.
- UNFCCC convention for climate change control, signed June 11, 1992, ratified November 12, 1993 and put into action March 21, 1994.
- Stockholm Convention/POPs, signed January 18, 2002 and ratified November 8, 2004

Case study

The pharmaceutical industry in Jordan is an important player in the local economy as it is one of the main export industries and an influential employment generator. This importance is affirmed by its rank as the second-highest Jordanian exporter (JD 353 million in 2008), positioning it as the first true leading industry in Jordan (Jordan Association of Pharmaceutical Manufacturers (JAPM), 2010). The high quality, splendid reputation and affordable price of Jordanian pharmaceutical products led this industry, in 2005, to export 70 per cent of its sales to more than 60 countries, including the EU and USA, with earnings of JD 198.6 million (JAPM, 2010).

Table 6.2 Sources of Emissions in Jordan

Source	Pollutants	Area
Petroleum refinery	CO, CO_2, H_2S, SO_2 and hydrocarbons	Zarqa
Hussein thermal power plant, vehicles, etc.	CO, CO_2, SO_2, and NO_x	Zarqa and Kingdom-wide
▶ Cement factories; ▶ phosphate mines; ▶ phosphate and potash loading; ▶ loading and discharging at crop silos.	Dust	▶ Fuheis, Adasiya, Dhuleil; ▶ Ruseifa, Hasa, Shadiya, Abyad; ▶ Aqaba; ▶ Aqaba.
▶ Industrial estates; ▶ steel and iron factories, leather tanning, chemical detergents and batteries.	Cl_2, F_2, Pb_2, SO_2, CO	▶ Amman, Ruseifa, Awajan, Zarqa, Sahab; ▶ Kingdom-wide.

Table 6.2   (Continued)

Source	Pollutants	Area
Quarries and asphalt mixing	Dust, CO, CO_2, SiO_2	N/A
Fires, waste and grass burning, tire burning.	CO, CO_2	N/A
Fertilizer plant	F_2, NH_3, SO_2	Aqaba
▶ Glass factory; ▶ bakeries; ▶ power plant.	CO, CO_2, SO_2	▶ Ma'an ▶ All areas ▶ Marka
Treatment plants	Odor, H_2S, NH_3, CH_4	Khirbet Assamra, others
Potash plant	Dust, SO_2, CO_2	Ghor Safi
▶ Crude oil loading; ▶ petrol station.	Hydrocarbons	▶ Aqaba ▶ Kingdom-wide

Source: State of Cleaner Production in Jordan, report prepared by Land and Human to Advocate Progress (LHAP), SMAP Clearing House (2008). http://smap.ew.eea.europa.eu/fol112686/fol030856/fol912729/state-cleaner-production-jordan

A study was performed on two representative pharmaceutical plants (A and B) to evaluate their environmental performance and to examine CER in the Jordanian pharmaceutical sector. In both plants, the CP approach was employed to provide cost-effective and environmentally friendly alternatives to the current situation.

The collection of processes and site data helped to provide a better understanding of the processes that generate waste in both case studies. This was done through preparing flow diagrams for some processes to identify losses or emissions of the waste streams. These processes were chosen with consensus from the management of both companies, where they were inspected and analyzed to identify suspected sources of waste. After that a set of comprehensive CP options was generated. These options were subjected to a full technical and economic feasibility study. Options that seemed to be impractical were eliminated from further consideration.

These two case studies resulted in the identification of four CP options for plant A, with two of them selected as the most feasible, and option 1 resulted in saving more than JD 275,000 a year (Table 6.3). On the other hand, seven CP options were identified at

Table 6.3 Most Feasible Clean Production Options for Plant A

Clean production option	Environmental benefits
Option 1: recovery unit for acetone from API X and Y.	210,750 kg/year; savings JD 278,445; estimated investment JD 100,000; pay back after five months.
Option 2: use waste solvent for wet cleaning instead of purified water.	Reduction in water consumption.

Table 6.4 Most Feasible Clean Production Options for Plant B

Clean production option	Environmental benefits
Option 1: wrapping upper opening of milling machine with plastic shrink films.	Reduce dust generation.
Option 2: Venturi Jet.	Reduce powder spills and dust; minimize production time.
Option 3: selling solid waste disposables to a local recycling company.	Save natural resources.
Option 4: recycling reverse osmosis water.	Water saving 3120 m³/year; saving JD 5740/year.
Option 5: selling plant remnants as soil additive to farmers, or selling them to a local company for composting.	900–1200 kg/year

plant B, and five of them were selected as the most feasible. Option 4 resulted in a saving of more than JD 5500 a year (Table 6.4).

Plant A is capable of manufacturing a wide range of active pharmaceutical ingredients (APIs) by chemical synthesis, through utilizing many types of chemical reactions, recovery processes and chemical substances. Different APIs are produced with different rates. APIs X and Y are the only two that are manufactured repeatedly and with huge amounts.

The raw materials used in plant A can be classified into two categories: reactants and solvents. The names of reactants were not allowed to be known by any party other than employees and operators working at this plant, for the reason that the production formula of any API is confidential.

The manufacturing process of an API is mainly a chemical reaction. Several reactants enter a chemical reactor, where a chemical reaction takes place under strict conditions. The resulting stream is composed of the API and different by-products. This stream enters different recovery processes, for which solvents are used to help separate the API from the by-products.

As the solvents enter into the recovery processes, by-products are dissolved in them, and then they get out as waste streams with almost the same amount that they entered with. The main solvent used in the manufacturing of both X and Y APIs is acetone. The estimated generated amount of acetone waste is 210,750 kg a year. Under current management practices, this extremely large amount of acetone waste is transported off-site to a local landfill under the supervision of the Jordan Ministry of Environment. In addition to the purchasing cost, plant A pays around JD 95,150 a year in disposal fees, which is a substantial financial burden on the company.

The first option that must be taken into consideration is pollution prevention. It is defined by the US Environmental Protection Agency (USEPA, 1991) as a strategy that emphasizes reducing the amount of pollution or waste created, rather than controlling waste or dealing with pollutants after they have been created. Minimizing solvents at the source requires modifying the manufacturing processes of API X and Y. This could be done through conducting a dedicated research program to investigate a new method or develop the current method of manufacturing to consume fewer solvents, especially acetone.

The next option is about reusing waste solvents. The strict quality control requirements of the pharmaceutical industry often restrict reuse opportunities, though some do exist. After a high degree of purification, materials recovered from manufacturing processes may be reused (USEPA, 1991). The most feasible alternative is to install a recovery unit, such as a distillation column, to purify and reuse them. Applying this option substantially reduces the disposal fee and the cost of purchasing the acetone, therefore saving around JD 280,000 annually. This requires an estimated initial investment of JD 100,000 (Table 6.3).

Solvents from various industries in Jordan are always transported to local landfills under supervision of the Ministry of Environment. Instead of storing these huge amounts of solvents for a long time in landfill sites, it is recommended that they are incinerated, thus using them as a source of energy. A flue gas control unit could be added to control all possible air contamination from such solvents.

Plant B produces a wide range of finished pharmaceutical dosage forms. Each one is composed of both an API and excipients. Plant B is also engaged in the manufacturing of a type of API based on natural product extraction in a herbal facility. Large waste volumes from the plant remnants are produced (900–1200 kg a year), due to the fact that the amount of finished API is always small compared with the amount of natural source used. The extraction process utilized at plant B is old, thus it consumes a lot of the natural products and generates two-thirds of the input as waste. This process is now undergoing thorough research and development in order to upgrade it to be more efficient and to give higher product yields.

After extracting the API, the extract is delivered to the general formulation facility, where it is formulated in the semi-solid department as ointments and suppositories. Under current management practices, the plant waste that is generated is transported off-site to a local landfill under the supervision of the Ministry of Environment.

A simple, yet very effective, alternative is to sell these remnants to a local composting company, which will process the waste and convert it to compost. It is also applicable to use these remnants as a soil additive without further processing and composting, thus selling them to farmers directly. In addition to the profit generated from selling the plant remnants, this option saves the company from paying the disposal fee. This alternative is considered a good example of industrial ecology. Industrial ecology involves actions taken to reduce the industrial system's impact on the environment; in particular, creating a closed industrial system, analogous to a natural ecosystem, where waste from one industry can be used by another (O'Rourke et al., 1996; Erkman, 1997).

The water treatment unit at plant B is used to produce acceptable pharmaceutical-grade water for drug formulation. The minimum-quality water specified by the US Pharmacopeia to enter the treatment process is drinking water, which passes through several filters, a softener, ultraviolet light and reverse osmosis membranes to produce low total dissolved solids (TDS) pharmaceutical-grade water (WHO, 2005). The water treatment unit rejects a huge amount of water, around 12 m^3 a day, which is discharged into the sewers.

An effective alternative to rejecting the waste water is to recover and recycle it back to the 1400 m^3 municipal drinking-water tank available at the facility. The rejected water was analyzed for its TDS and found to have an average of 421 mg of TDS per liter. This rejected water can be diluted with the municipal drinking water, even if it has a higher TDS, keeping it within the accepted drinking-water standards. Recycling the water rejected during treatment as municipal drinking water saves around 3120 m^3 of water each year and JD 5740 annually. Although this amount of saving is not significant for developed countries, it is of considerable importance for a country like Jordan, which is a poor country in terms of water resources (Table 6.4).

Critical analysis and discussions

All the initiatives carried out in Jordan in the past, and the results of the study on the assessment of CER in the Jordanian private sector with respect to the UN GC (UNDP, 2007), unfortunately show that there is no clear understanding regarding GC, CSR, CER, CP and environmentally friendly technology programs by Jordanian companies in different sectors. Although some corporations in different sectors in Jordan have adopted various voluntary initiatives in socially responsible business and environment practices, there is still a need for more strategic focus and long-term sustainability. Hence, the understanding of environmental management and friendly technologies and processes is still minimal; few large companies try to demonstrate that they have a positive impact on the environment. Also, the UNDP study concluded that Jordanian companies' social responsibility activities fall short of expectations and are mostly cosmetic. Results also indicated that profit is the most important goal for business organizations. Furthermore, the natural environment has consistently been underrated in the list of challenges from the private sector, despite growing evidence related to the endemic problems of water scarcity, air pollution and climate change. The companies least concerned with environmental issues are those operating in sectors with higher environmental risks (UNDP, 2007).

Also, the UNDP study found that the awareness level of the managers of enterprises is nominal due to a lack of concern of the necessity of such practices. Saving money and having a good image are the greatest motivations for using environmentally friendly technology. A lack of government incentives, awareness, guidance on CSR and CER, and the high cost of implementing CSR are the challenges that face the implementation of CSR in Jordanian companies, as well as a lack of quantitative performance indicators to evaluate the CER activities in the company. Market drivers for CER are relatively weak in Jordan; there is a virtual absence of media, clients and consumer pressures. And a qualitative discussion on the language of CER and the important issues for Jordan is generally missing from academic and business literature.

Suwaidan et al. (2004) found, on average, that only 13 per cent of the items included in the index of social responsibility disclosure practices in the annual reports of Jordanian industrial companies. The results revealed that there is a fairly good level of disclosure of human resources and community involvement information, while there is a poor level of disclosure of environmental and goods/services to customers. The fact that the legal social and environmental disclosure requirements for reporting are few in Jordan means that substantial attention and legal reform should be given to sustainable reporting.

The only dedicated association and representative body for the pharmaceutical industry in Jordan is The Jordanian Association of Pharmaceutical Manufacturers (JAPM), which was established in 1996. This association plays a big role in developing and upgrading the Jordanian pharmaceutical industry to world-class competitive standards (JAPM, 2010). However, JAPM is still in the early stages of introducing and prompting corporate responsibility (CR) to the pharmaceutical companies. The corporate sector should have policies or an organized action plan to divide the role of companies in each sector, where each company knows in advance what to do in terms of its CSR and CER obligations.

Currently there are 16 pharmaceutical manufacturers in Jordan. Only two of them mention CR on their websites. The first one has a very descriptive and thorough CR page, publishing its own annual CR reports that contain social and environmental performance in all aspects. The second company shows a very promising, yet brief, description of their environmental policy. A lack of reporting ensures that Jordanian CSR is under-represented both locally and internationally. What is needed in this respect is greater transparency of CSR initiatives, improved measuring, sustainable reporting and professional auditing.

Based on the information provided in this section we can conclude that in Jordan, CSR as an institutionalized concept is still very much in the early stages of its development. Most companies do not have CSR programs incorporated into their structure. Yet CSR is gaining prominence in the business community as traditional notions of charitable giving combine with Western-style social responsibility and environmental standards. This will lead us to work on identifying how to encourage more Jordanian companies to adopt CSR as part of their business culture.

Corporations tend to donate their money to services and material assistance, such as supporting orphanages and hospitals, rather than to more long-term causes like saving the environment or funding research. They believe that this will help them to build their reputation faster, as people need to eat and have houses before protecting the biosphere. The notion of philanthropy is often confused with CSR in Jordan.

Lessons and implications for top managers, policy makers and governments

Although the government is trying to support a few initiatives implemented yearly in Jordan, the role of the private sector and the impact of their CSR behaviors is still minimal. Efforts are ineffective, insufficient and accordingly the role of the private sector in development is deficient. Most Jordanian companies lack knowledge and an awareness of CER. Therefore, a deeper understanding of the role of the private sector is needed, and both small- and large-scale enterprises should be encouraged to embed CSR in their business.

The private sector should be aware that it is part of the development cycle and should work cooperatively with the government. The relationship between the government, the private sector and civil society needs to be strengthened in Jordan. One way of doing this is for the government to encourage CER by providing tax exemptions for those who implement such initiatives. Religious leaders and scholars can elevate people's priorities from mere charity to development causes. NGOs can cooperate with the government to promote the CSR concept, using media campaigns to introduce this approach and encourage corporations to contribute to development initiatives.

Unfortunately, the environment is not viewed as a priority by most Jordanian companies. Private-sector awareness of Jordanian environment legislation is weak. A lack of public and government attention to environmental issues is met with a lack of proactive effort from the private sector. Government policies that promote environmental management, with an emphasis on pollution prevention as the first step in reducing wastes, must be encouraged.

Referring to the Environmental Impact Assessment Order (no. 37/2005), unfortunately pharmaceutical industries in Jordan are excluded from conducting Environmental Impact Assessment (EIA). Revising and including pharmaceutical industries in the EIA order – categorizing lists and establishing EIA guidelines for pharmaceutical industries – will enhance and support the application of CER and CP. It is crucial for the Ministry of Environment to establish EIA guidelines for the pharmaceutical industry, which will be applied during the EIA assessment phase.

Jordanian companies are looking for models in this direction. Demonstration projects that show that the environmental and financial benefits of CP are applicable to enterprises in both developing countries and developed countries must be implemented. Institutions that can effectively implement CP programs based on process optimization must be supported; unfortunately, there are no incentives for the private sector to adopt environmentally friendly technologies.

The media, regulatory institutions/bodies and consumers as a pressure mechanism are not using their potential fully. Business will not care if the market does not care. For attitudes to change, the public must be made aware of the importance of this concept.

Summary and recommendations

Even though there is strong desire among business leaders to contribute to the development needs of the country, one of the challenges observed for Jordanian companies is the need to organize their CSR approaches effectively. Current activities, mostly in the form of charity, lack long-term sustainability and strategic focus. Consequently, companies need to be more systematic and strategic about CSR. A systematic process of identifying and prioritizing the social and environmental agenda is needed, as well as a shift of focus from 'giving' to 'impact'.

The Jordanian government needs to establish a solid framework for efficient operation and growth to be followed by the private sector. This includes ensuring efficient market regulations, fair competition and the protection of workers' rights. There is also a need to upgrade and enforce environmental legislation and regulation to enhance the environmental performance of the private sector. Attention should be paid to the sustainable reporting and auditing which represent the CSR of Jordanian companies in international benchmark studies and indices. Economic incentives for the implementation of CER practices need to be shaped. In addition, the private sector has the opportunity to work beyond this framework and to commit itself deeply to social and environmental issues. Recruiting CSR/CER specialists in each corporation will enhance the development and implementation of strategic CSR.

Furthermore, efforts toward CSR, CER, pollution prevention and control are needed to meet international standards. This could be reflected in the permit system, with the inclusion of ISO 26000 and cleaner technologies as a prerequisite, and with further support to the CP program so that it can boost CER and CP activities and projects more widely across the country.

Another recommendation is to expand the role of business unions, Jordanian Industrial Chambers, syndicates, research centers and other civil society institutions to support the activities of CER in Jordan. For example, the development of guides and training toolkits, the dissemination of information and success stories, and a code of conduct for CSR activities in Jordan could be considered as guidelines for future CSR action by Jordanian companies. Evaluating the CER activities of Jordanian companies, key quantitative performance indicators or standards of CER could be set as part of corporate governance rules. Such indicators are useful when comparing the CER actions of different Jordanian companies, and between Jordanian firms and foreign companies in similar countries.

To move forward, this study highlights a number of areas where Jordanian companies need to pay greater attention:

- Networking, training and the dissemination of information and success stories through the media will serve to promote CSR awareness in Jordan.
- Companies need to be more strategic in their CSR and environmental activities.
- The government and public authorities have an important role to play by enabling better framework conditions for the CSR movement to evolve and have a positive impact on the lives of the Jordanian people.

References

Brand, L. A. (1998) *Women: The State and Political Liberalization: Middle Eastern and North Africa Experience*. Columbia University Press, New York, p. 320.

Burton Hamner, W. (1996) *What Is the Relationship among Cleaner Production, Pollution Prevention, Waste Minimisation and ISO 14000?* Paper presented at the First Asian Conference on Cleaner Production in the Chemical Industry. Taipei, Taiwan.

Department of Statistics of Jordan (2008) *Appraisal of Poverty Indicators Based on the Household Expenditure Survey*. Department of Statistics, Jordan.

Elian, K. (2005) *The State of Corporate Social Responsibility in Jordan: Case Studies from Major Business Sectors*. The Fifth Mediterranean Development Forum MDF5, Strengthening Responsible Corporate Citizenship in Business MENA Region.

Emerging Jordan & American Chamber of Commerce (2005) *Jordan Country Profile, Emerging Market Series*. Oxford Business Group, Oxford.

Environmental Protection Agency (EPA) (2000) *A Self-Help Tool for Small to Medium-Sized Businesses*. Department of State and Regional Development (NSW), New South Wales. Version 1. ISBN 0 7313 2736 5, EPA 2000/50.

Erkman, S. (1997) 'Industrial Ecology: A Historical View', *Journal of Cleaner Production*, 5 (1–2), 1–10.

Hohnen, P. (2007) *CSR: An Implementation Guide for Business*. Editor Jason Potts, International Institute for Sustainable Development, ISBN 978-1-895536-97-3.

International Labour Organization (ILO) (1998) *Declaration on Fundamental Principles and Rights at Work*. United Nations International Labour Organisation. http://www.ilo.org/declaration/thedeclaration/textdeclaration/lang–en/index.htm

International Standard Organisation (2010) *ISO 26000: Guidance on Social responsibility*. International Standard Organisation, Switzerland, Geneva.

ISO 14001 (series) *Environmental Management Systems – Requirements with Guidance for Use*. International Standard Organisation, Switzerland, Geneva.

Jordan Association of Pharmaceutical Manufacturers (JAPM) (2010) *Pharmaceutical Industry Bank*. JAPM in cooperation with European Union and Jordan Enterprise Development Corporation (JEDCO), Jordan.

O'Rourke, D., L. Connelly, and C. P. Koshland (1996) 'Industrial Ecology – A Critical Review', *International Journal of Environmental Pollution*, 6 (2–3), 89–112.

SMAP Clearing House (2008) *Euro-Mediterranean Programme for the Environment: State of Cleaner Production in Jordan*. The report is prepared by Land and Human to Advocate Progress (LHAP) in the framework of an assignment of SMAP RMSU project, contributor Ruba Anbar.

Suwaidan, M., M. Al-omari, and R. H. Haddad (2004) 'Social Responsibility Disclosure and Corporate Characteristics: The Case of Jordanian Industrial Companies', *International Journal of Accounting, Auditing and Performance Evaluation*, 1 (4), 432–447.

UNDP (2003) *Human development Report 2003: Millennium Development Goals: A compact among nations to end human poverty*. Published for the United Nations Development Program (UNDP), Oxford University Press, New York, Oxford.

UNDP (2007) *UN Global Compact: Assessment of Corporate Environmental Responsibility in Jordan*. Prepared by Muna Y. Hindiyeh. http://www.undp-jordan.org/Portals/0/GC%20Environment%20report.doc

UN Global Compact (2007) *An Inspirational Guide to Implementing the UN Global Compact*. Global Compact Network, Ukraine. http://www.globalcompact.org.ua/rcenter/resources/25

United Nations (UN) (1948) *Universal Declaration of Human Rights*. United Nations General Assembly. http://www.un.org/en/documents/udhr/

United Nations Conference on Environment and Development (1992) *Rio Declaration on Environment and Development*. Rio de Janeiro. http://www.un.org/documents/ga/conf151/aconf15126-1annex1.htm

US Environmental Protection Agency (USEPA) (1991) *Guides to Pollution Prevention: The Pharmaceutical Industry*. EPA/625/7-9l/017.

WBCSD (2000) *Corporate Social Responsibility: Making Good Business Sense*. ISBN 2-940240-078.

WHO (2005) *Good Manufacturing Practices: Water for Pharmaceutical Use*. WHO Technical Report Series, No. 929.

Further reading, case studies and assistance

Eccles, R. G. and M. P. Krzus (2010) *One Report: Integrated Reporting for a Sustainable Strategy*. Wiley, Hoboken, NJ.

Global Report Initiative (2007) *Biodiversity: A GRI Reporting Resource*. ISBN 978-90-8866-001-6.

Hillary, R. (ed.) (1997) *Environmental Management Systems and Cleaner Production*. Wiley, New York.

Hopkins, M. (2007) *Corporate Social Responsibility and International Development: Is Business the Solution*. Earthscan, London, UK.

Jamison, A. (2005) *Defining Corporate Environmental Responsibility: Canadian ENGO Perspectives*. The Pembina Institute and Pollution Probe. Canada.

Mulholland, K. L. (2006) *Identification of Cleaner Production: Improvement Opportunities*. Wiley-AlChE, Hoboken, NJ, p. 200.

Quano, E. A. (2009) *Cleaner Production: Myth and Reality*. VDM Verlag, Saarbrücken, Germany, p. 324.

Richards, D. J. (ed.) (1997) *The Industrial Green Game: Implications for Environmental Design and Management*. National Academy Press, Washington, DC, USA, ISBN 0-309-05294-7.

Schaltegger, S., M. Bennett, and R. L. Burritt (2008) *Environmental Management Accounting for Cleaner Production*. Springer, p. 500. http://www.springer.com/business+%26+management/accounting/book/978-1-4020-8912-1

Schwartz, M. S. (2011) *Corporate Social Responsibility: An Ethical Approach. Broadview. Perspectives*. The Pembina Institute and Pollution Probe, Canada.

Suh, S. (ed.) (2009) *Handbook of Input-Output Economics in Industrial Ecology*. Springer. ISBN 978-1402061547

UNEP (1998) *Cleaner Production: A Guide to Sources of Information*. Paris: UNEP IE, p. 44.

Werther, W. B. and D. Chandler (2010) *Strategic Corporate Social Responsibility: Stakeholders in a global environment*. SAGE Publications, Thousand Oaks, CA, p. 415.

Willis, A. (2003) 'The Role of the Global Reporting Initiative's Sustainability Reporting Guidelines in the Social Screening of Investments', *Journal of Business Ethics* 43 (3), 233–237.

7
The Development of CSR Reporting in the Middle East

Jeannette Vinke and Aida El-Khatib

Introduction

Corporate social responsibility (CSR) has been gaining importance globally over the last few years, as numerous supporters have advocated its integration into day-to-day business practices and many researchers have advocated the business case for doing so (Vogel, 2005; Gray et al., 2010). Aside from financial performance reporting, there has been renewed interest in recent years in social performance reporting, or what is commonly referred to as CSR reporting. CSR in the Middle East is generally considered to be lagging behind CSR practice in more developed economies (Al-Khater and Naser, 2003; Mezher et al., 2010). The peculiar socio-economic landscape of the Middle East region implies that the forces that both drive and hinder CSR are unique to this region as well (Mezher et al., 2010).

In this chapter we aim to provide an overview of the current status of CSR reporting in the Middle East, as well as set the next phase for CSR reporting in the region. The research presented in this chapter therefore relies heavily on secondary sources, particularly books and scholarly articles. Given the scarcity of literature on CSR in the Middle East, we also draw here on our own CSR-related research and experiences. We begin with an overview of the current status of CSR reporting globally, followed by an in-depth analysis of CSR and how it is reported in the Middle East. An elaborate case study analyzing CSR reporting in the United Arab Emirates (UAE) is followed by two examples of regional CSR reporting initiatives. We conclude by determining the need for a distinct Middle Eastern perspective on CSR reporting. As such, the chapter will be of interest to academics as well as to practitioners looking to deepen their understanding of CSR reporting activities in the region.

CSR reporting globally

As defined by the United Nations, sustainability refers to 'development that meets the need of present generations without compromising the ability of future generations to meet their needs' (Visser et al., 2010, p. 384). Sustainability can thus be incorporated into every element of life, from corporate production to individual consumption to societal development. CSR is seen to be a subset of sustainability, referring to the actions an organization takes to minimize the negative impacts of its actions on the environment and on society. CSR is comprehensive, encompassing 'the economic, legal, ethical, and discretionary or philanthropic expectations that society has of organizations at a given point in time' (Visser et al., 2010, p. 107). Society does not only expect organizations to embed CSR into their practices, but also expect organizations to report their CSR-related activities and practices. CSR and sustainability are increasingly used interchangeably (Gray et al., 2010). In line with the rest of the book, this chapter will use the term 'CSR' unless quoting authors that use the term 'sustainability'.

The reporting of CSR practices should be in line with the expectations and requirements of various internal and external stakeholders. From an internal stakeholder perspective, and to truly embed CSR in the core of any organization, it is necessary to measure all activities that have social, environmental and economic impacts. Since CSR reporting has recently gained importance internationally, there are no set models to ensure that these impacts are properly measured and reported internally. However, efforts to develop such models are under way, with pioneering companies across the world currently experimenting with internal CSR reporting models such as CSR Key performance indicators (KPIs), balanced scorecards and other strategic measurement tools (Figge et al., 2002; Snider et al., 2003). As these models become more routinely used by organizations, their success in capturing the full impact of business activities can be gauged. As such, we can expect further progress in this area in the future.

One model that we believe addresses the full impact of business activities is the Sustainability Decision-Making Model (Hopwood et al., 2010). This model, which has been developed by Accounting for Sustainability (A4S), embeds sustainability internally through consideration of economic, environmental and social impacts along three phases covering the 'product or service range', the 'specific product or service' and the 'balanced decision' ('Sustainability Decision-Making Model', 2010) (Figure 7.1).

The first phase involves reviewing the entire product or service range to assess its full impact and also whether the impact is in line with the firm's sustainability objectives. The second phase involves detailing the economic, environmental and social impacts of specific products and services, including their specific supply chains. The analysis in this phase considers how these impacts fit in with the general impacts identified in the first phase of the model, as well as with the firm's sustainability objectives. The third phase involves making fully informed decisions on a product-by-product basis as to how to improve its impact financially, environmentally and socially

A market-based approach to sustainability

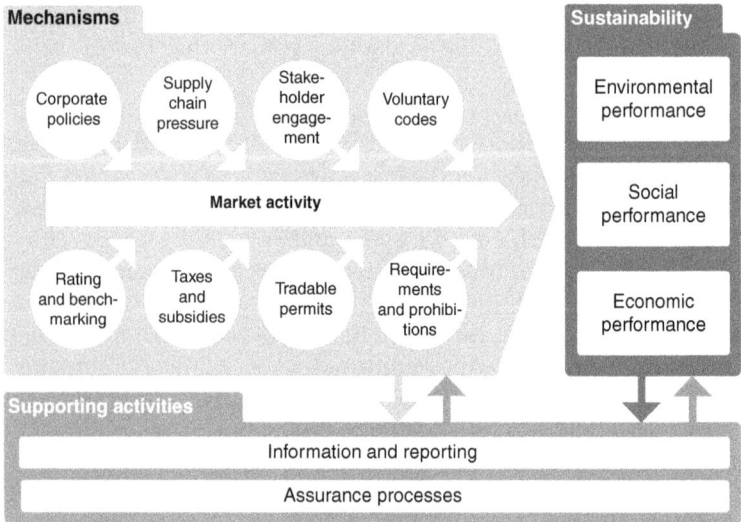

Figure 7.1 Sustainability   Decision-Making   Model   (Accounting   for Sustainability, 2010)

Source: Reproduced with the permission of Accounting for Sustainability.

('Sustainability Decision-Making Model', 2010). The model, through its three phases, ensures that sustainability is considered along the life cycle, supply chain and formal decision-making ('Sustainability Decision-Making Model', 2010).

From an external stakeholder perspective (Boesso and Michelon, 2010; Burrit and Schaltegger, 2010), it has now become a common standard for large global companies to include CSR-related disclosures in their annual report. Moreover, it is becoming increasingly common for firms to issue separate sustainability reports. About 68 per cent of the Global 250 firms prepared a separate annual sustainability report in 2004 (KPMG, 2005). However, while financial reporting and disclosures are governed by legislation around the world, there is no legislation governing the content and format of CSR-related reporting, whether it is part of the annual report or is separately reported (Dilling, 2010). Efforts are being made on this front, of which Global Reporting Initiative (GRI) is prominent. GRI is a network-based organization that has developed what is believed to be one of the most widely used guidelines for external sustainability reporting. Its detailed guidelines cover aspects such as content and report boundary, are universally applicable and comparable across size, industry and geographical location, and continuously evolve to reflect the reporting needs of stakeholders.

GRI guidelines were first developed in 1996 as a CSR reporting framework that is applicable across countries, sectors and business sizes (Brown et al., 2009; 'What is GRI?', 2011). The framework is developed and improved based on input from various stakeholders, and sets out 'principles and indicators that organizations can use to measure and report their economic, environmental and social performance' in a universally standardized manner ('What is GRI?', 2011). The guidelines provide the foundation for CSR reporting, and are accompanied by protocols, sector supplements and national protocols that assist firms in reporting the content that is most applicable to their country and business arena (Thurm, 2006). GRI guidelines are particularly detailed and cover report content, quality and boundary ('What are the G3 Guidelines?', 2011). A typical GRI sustainability report is detailed in nature and includes a 'CEO statement, profile of the reporting organizations, an executive summary and key indicators, vision and strategy, policies organization, and management systems and performance' (Reynolds and Yuthas, 2008, p. 53). The

Guidelines require the sustainability report to be audited, and the current rating system rates the CSR disclosures of an organization on three levels, where an application rating disclosed by an organization is affirmed through GRI's review and an external auditor's review.

In addition to GRI, a list of the more important international reporting standards and frameworks is shown in Table 7.1.

International CSR reporting and standards are not homogenous and hence not comparable at the moment (Aerts and Cormier, 2009). Since shareholders and other stakeholders are increasingly demanding transparency globally, as is the case with institutional investors demanding clear CSR-related disclosures (Scholtens, 2006), CSR reporting is expected to gain prominence. Moreover, as guidelines are used more often and universally, comparability and a common format for CSR reports will likely emerge.

Table 7.1 International CSR Reporting Standards and Frameworks

---

EMAS (European environmental management and audit)
The Eco Management and Audit Scheme is a 'voluntary environmental management system' through which firms improve their environmental monitoring and reporting ('Summary', 2011). Its core elements are 'performance, credibility, and transparency' ('Summary', 2011). It aims to 'recognize and reward organizations that go beyond minimum environmental legal requirements and continuously improve their environmental performance' (Visser, Matten, Pohl & Tolhurst, 2010, p. 146).

ISO 14001 (Internationally recognized environmental management certification)
ISO 14001 is a voluntary environmental management system standard that was issued by The International Organization for Standardization. ISO 14001 focuses on the organization's processes rather than its products and services. It encompasses 'organizational structure, planning activities, responsibilities, practices, procedures, processes and resources for developing, implementing, achieving, reviewing and maintaining the environmental policy' (Visser, Matten, Pohl & Tolhurst, 2010, p. 250).

SA8000 (Social Accountability International labor standard)
SA8000 is a social accountability standard that focuses on universal fair labor practices. It is an 'auditable certification standard' developed from 'the International Labor Organization's conventions, the Universal Declaration of Human Rights and the UN Convention on the Rights of the Child' ('SA8000 Standard', 2010). The SA8000's main elements include child labor, forced labor, health and safety, freedom of association and right to collective bargaining, discrimination, discipline, working hours, compensation and management systems ('SA8000 Standard', 2010).

Drivers and hindrances of CSR reporting in the Middle East

Even though CSR has long been embedded in the way Middle Eastern organizations do business, according to our research, which will be discussed later on, the general level of awareness of CSR and understanding of its business implications appears to be limited. There is a lack of academic research on CSR reporting in the region, with our own literature review on CSR reporting research in the Gulf Cooperation Council (GCC) (conducted in 2010) yielding only three papers.

Rettab et al. (2008) investigated the perception of companies concerning CSR's impact on the organization's financial performance, employee performance and corporate reputation. They found that CSR, on the whole, had a positive impact on all three aspects. Mezher et al. (2010) looked at CSR in the renewable energy sector and provided examples from the Masdar Initiative in Abu Dhabi. The paper describes how the Emirate of Abu Dhabi has been taking bold steps to become a regional leader in renewable energy. This indicates that thoughts about the long-term sustainability of the region are being taken seriously, with both environmental issues and social issues being addressed. Masdar City, for instance, aims to provide more skilled job opportunities for local Emiratis. Abu Dhabi has included environmental goalposts in its new long-term vision (Abu Dhabi 2030). Despite successfully describing the elements above, Mezher et al.'s paper fails to address the wider issues that are beyond the Government of Abu Dhabi and Masdar City. The paper brushes over the remaining challenges that 'include cultural differences, low consumer interest, and other challenges that are common in developing countries' (Mezher et al., 2010, p. 758). Al-Khater and Naser's (2003) study of Qatar explored the perceptions of social responsibility and accountability in Qatar's financial sector. The study found that participants agreed that CSR should generally be encouraged, and that the disclosure of CSR activities by companies would serve society at large. However, the study does not provide any indication of the current level of CSR disclosure in Qatar.

In an attempt to gauge the Middle Eastern CSR model, we have conducted research that was originally based on the market-based approach model to sustainability (2004) of the Institute of Chartered

Inputs	Outcomes	Decisions

Phase 1 – Reviewing the sustainability impacts of the products or service range

Product or service life-cycle		Prioritise sustainability issues for improvement
Sustainability issues	Mapping of potential sustainability impacts	Identify areas to drive change with suppliers
		Identify areas for further research
Stakeholders' expectations		Strengthen the organisation's sustainability policy and management framework
Organisational policies		Strengthen the organisation's understanding of stakeholders' expectations

Phase 2 – Analysing the sustainability impacts of a specific product or service

Product or service specific life-cycle		Agree on supplier and product or service life-cycle sustainability rating
Supplier's sustainability context	Sustainability rating for a product's or service's life-cycle and action plan for improvement	Identify improvement actions for each supplier within the product or service life-cycle
Sustainability issues and likely impact		Identify costs related to improving the product's or service's sustainability
Organisational policies		

Phase 3 – Reaching a balanced and informed decision as to how the product's or service's sustainability performance can be improved

Product life-cycle supplier sustainability rating		Decide which components to buy at what sustainability quality, cost and business befefit
Other product and supplier parameters	Improved product or service sustainability performance	Decide to encourage suppliers' improvement of their sustainability performance
Consumer and other stakeholders' buying behaviours		Decide to engage with consumers, demonstrate the value of sustainability products, and encourage change in consumption patterns
Organisation's sustainability strategy and policy		

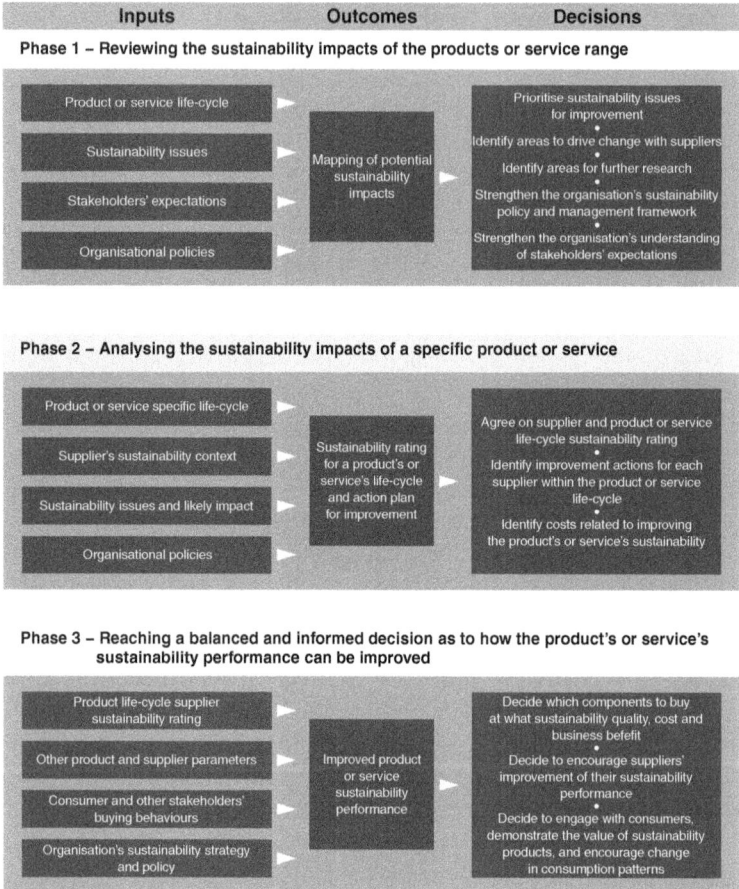

Figure 7.2   Market-Based Approach Model
Source: Reproduced with permission of the ICAEW, Sustainability: the role of accountants, ICAEW (2004).

Accountants in England and Wales (ICAEW) (Figure 7.2). ICAEW's model argues that:

- by incorporating sustainability into their core corporate policies, companies increase the opportunities for improved corporate governance and competitive advantage;
- purchasers and buyers promote a desired standard of sustainability among others in their supply chain (supply chain pressure);

- with stakeholder engagement, those with a particular influence can engage in dialog, provide feedback and influence the actions of a company;
- voluntary codes encourage organizations to improve certain aspects concerning the sustainability of their actions;
- rating and benchmarking organizations rank them on the basis of their sustainability performance;
- financial incentives such as taxes and subsidies encourage corporations to behave more sustainably;
- by mandating tradable permits, governments limit certain activities or resources to improve sustainability;
- through requirements and prohibitions, governments and authorities can enforce positive steps or limit unsustainable actions;
- through CSR information and reporting activities, companies communicate both internally and externally the operations of their mechanisms to promote sustainable development;
- assurance policies help organizations prove the legitimacy of their actions toward sustainable development (i.e. environmental, social and economic performance).

Using the market-based approach model as a base, we tested its validity through interviewing ten professionals who deal with CSR strategies and CSR reporting in the UAE. This original research is published for the first time here.

Research methodology

The individuals were chosen after an extensive media search, finding companies that dealt with CSR extensively. No interview requests were rejected. Eight of the interviews were face-to-face, lasting 60 minutes or more. Two interviews were over the phone, lasting between 40 and 60 minutes. All interviews were taped and transcribed with the permission of the interviewees. The background of CSR was reviewed before the interviews along with interviewees' submitted biographies and other relevant information. The interviewer supplied basic background information concerning the research (which included a copy of ICAEW's market-based approach model) and a basic agenda before each interview was carried out. All interviewees indicated their willingness to receive further questions

Table 7.2   Interviewee Information

Interview No.	Industry	Job Title	CSR Experience
1	Semi-Government	CSR Training Manger	CSR Training and Development for UAE companies
2	Private, Engineering firm	Director	Responsible for product innovation and business development in alternative energy/water saving
3	Private, Audit & Consulting	Partner	Consulting and Audit of Small and Medium Enterprises in the UAE
4	Semi-Government	Associate	CSR Coordinator in a CSR Department of a Chamber of Commerce
5	Private, Audit & Consulting	Partner	Responsible for CSR consulting
6	Semi-Government	Managing Director	In charge of local chapter of World Business Council for Sustainable Development
7	Semi-Government	Senior CSR Content Specialist	Designing CSR Education Strategies and material
8	Private, Audit & Consulting	Partner	Responsible for CSR Reporting and other consulting services
9	Private, Audit & Consulting	Manager	Responsible for Corporate Citizenship in the Middle East
10	Private, Audit & Consulting	Partner	Responsible for CSR consulting

by phone or e-mail. Four interviews were subsequently followed up by phone with clarification questions.

Basic information concerning the interviewees is described in Table 7.2.

The interviews were fairly open, with some structure provided through the following questions, which all of the interviewees were asked:

1. What does the interviewee believe in the current state of CSR in the UAE?
2. What drives CSR?
3. What hinders CSR?
4. How does ownership structure affect CSR?
5. What cultural aspects affect CSR and how do they affect?
6. Discussion of the applicability of the market-based approach model to sustainability from the ICAEW to the current UAE environment.
7. Any other ideas the interviewee would like to share.

Interview results

The results will be discussed as follows:

First, the applicability and the limitations of the eight drivers and their support activities identified in the market-based approach will be discussed. Second, further drivers and obstacles will be discussed, which will lead to the indicative conclusion concerning the current status of CSR in the UAE. An indicative model will be developed for UAE-specific drivers and obstacles concerning CSR.

Reactions to the market-based approach model

Corporate policies

Most interviewees were of the opinion that currently very few companies have embedded CSR in their corporate policies. Only those interviewees dealing with larger organizations were able to name some examples of companies that had moved to the stage where CSR was no longer just the 'icing on the cake' but formed part of their core strategy. These organizations were all operating internationally and had developed their CSR strategy partly through supply chain pressure. Notably, a few large companies in the tourist sector had found that to attract international business they had to prove their CSR credibility. As one interviewee put it:

> They told me that tour-operators from Western Europe all demanded written confirmation concerning their CSR policies, that triggered their initial action. They are now one of the leaders

in CSR in the region, and not only have they developed a number of initiatives, they now also measure these as part of their balanced scorecard.

On the whole, the company mentioned above appears to be an exception to the rule, and very few companies heed advice to make CSR part of their corporate policies. When talking about the whole Middle East and North Africa (MENA) region, a CSR champion at a consulting firm said:

> Many companies in the region are still struggling for survival. With this day-to-day pressure there is little bandwidth to think about longer term issues like sustainability.

An audit partner of a firm that is mainly involved with consulting and auditing small and medium enterprises (SMEs) in the region did not see CSR on the agenda of any of his clients:

> When something as basic as good corporate governance is still mainly 'seminar talk' it's clear that we are a far way from constructively looking at CSR.

Supply chain pressure

All interviewees noted that supply chain pressure is an increasingly important factor, although the pressure is almost exclusively from foreign companies onto local companies, but this appears to be limited to certain industries, like tourism.

One interviewee noted:

The UAE is still mainly a re-export market, not many goods are actually produced here, and hence supply-chain pressure is limited to only those companies who supply international clients.

Stakeholder engagement

When questioned about this, the stakeholders mentioned most, in order of frequency, were: consumers, employees and government. There was a general consensus of a lack of awareness among consumers:

> Nobody will ask you how many carbomiles a product has, or whether it was produced in ethical circumstances. A large part

of the population are uneducated labourers, they worry about sending money home, they don't care about CSR.

Many people are here on short-term visas, they are not concerned about the long-term well-being of the society.

Voluntary codes
None of the interviewees were aware of any voluntary codes.

Rating and benchmarking
Apart from a few initiatives, such as the CSR Arabia Awards and the CSR Label from the Dubai Chamber, none of the interviewees were aware of any rating or benchmarking available.

Taxes and subsidies
None of the interviewees were aware of any CSR-related taxes or subsidies. One interviewee remarked quite the opposite:

> Petrol is subsidized for all residents, and electricity and water for Emirati residents. This kind of subsidy encourages waste. The government does appear to be phasing out some of these subsidies though.

Tradable permits
None of the interviewees were aware of any tradable permits in place.

Requirement and prohibitions
One of the interviewees pointed out the Estidama Pearl Rating System (PRS) recently introduced by the Abu Dhabi government.

According to the website: 'It [the Estidama Pearl Rating System] is the Arab World's first sustainability rating system and is specifically tailored to the hot climate and arid environment of Abu Dhabi. The PRS has been designed to support sustainable development from design to construction to operational accountability' (Estidama Pearl Rating System, 2011).

Apart from this, the interviewees agree that the government's level of requirements and prohibitions is still low. One interviewee pointed out that:

> It is right at this stage not to enforce certain CSR activities. If these were legally mandatory, they wouldn't work. People would just try to implement the letter of the law without really understanding or making a genuine effort to be sustainable. We need to give these companies time to develop their sustainability strategies.

Support activities – information and reporting and the assurance process

The interviewees agreed that there is a general improvement, especially among larger, international companies, in the reporting of CSR activities. Very few companies requested external audits to be performed, but for selective international companies internal audits are being carried out.

How does ownership structure affect CSR?

Most of the interviewees agreed that the level of CSR interest was much greater where companies in the UAE were subsidiaries of international companies, especially large listed international companies:

> These corporations will have clear CSR corporate policies in place, which they will expect their subsidiaries to abide by. Often internal audits will enforce this behavior.

Not everybody agrees:

> International companies may sometimes forget their ethics when coming to this part of the world, would they consider treating their workers on construction sites in their home countries as they do here?

Most interviewees find that, although privately owned companies may be involved in charity, they are less likely to disclose these activities than listed companies:

> Many family owned businesses have very generous charity schemes, but they would not consider disclosing these activities,

it's not considered good to brag about charity in the Islamic tradition.

What drivers and obstacles are unique to the UAE?

When asked about the unique features of the UAE market that have an impact on CSR and related disclosures, interviewees mentioned: CSR awareness (10), culture (10), religion (7), expat population (6), emerging economy (4), lower education level and standard of living for a large part of the population (3), image (3), 'taboo topics' (2), CSR information not available in Arabic (2).

CSR Awareness is generally considered low. As one employee at a semi-government organization mentioned:

> For the last two years we no longer offered introductory courses to CSR, as we believed the market was ready to move on to more specific topics, we realized this was a mistake, there are still plenty of companies who belief that CSR is giving to charity and has nothing to do with business benefits.

Awareness does appear to be growing, though:

> Five years ago, nobody was thinking of CSR, even two years ago, it was more greenwashing than a genuine effort. That is changing, the financial crises has washed out those CSR professionals who were marketeers rather than anything else. Those of us that have survived are in it for the right reasons.

New CSR initiatives are popping up everywhere, it's a hot item and a lot of people are talking about it.

But also: 'Most companies, if asked about CSR, still think of it as an additional cost, something external to their environment, e.g. blood donation drives, cancer awareness walks, and contributions to World Wide Fund are the kind of activities that they will mention when asked about CSR' and 'We have a large percentage of expat laborers with low education levels struggling to send money back home. These people have no awareness and frankly do not care about this society as they are not integrated'.

The 'expat factor' seems to work both ways: 'Since the majority of people are here on short-term visas, they do not have a long-term

interest in this society. Change needs to come from the Emirati population, and we need to find ways to reach them.' But, 'we have expats
come in who are very aware and demand certain levels of CSR. They
may be used to giving up time voluntarily, recycle, or ask about the
ethics of a company. Other people learn from them and awareness
is increased'. On the other hand, 'a large group of expats come from
less developed countries, they may be educated, but often lack CSR
awareness. Littering for instance is the norm, and these norms are
imported into the UAE.'

Opinions are divided concerning cultural and religious traditions:
'I have seen no evidence of religious influence on CSR', but also 'the
duty to share and care in Islam is older than the western model
of CSR. Companies and individuals are used to paying *zakat*[1] and
sadqa[2] and see this as part of their obligation to society' and 'many
local companies are extremely charitable, however the religious and
cultural traditions call for them to be discrete about their givings.
They prefer not to disclose what they give away'. Another interviewee
said: 'Disclosing what you give in charity may look almost vulgar in
the islamic tradition where helping people discretely is worth more
than trumpeting about your good deeds. This contradicts the Western
model of transparency and disclosure around CSR.'

About image: 'Since the UAE wants to have a forward looking
image, the benefits of marketing good CSR have not gone unnoticed.'
And 'the pollution is destroying nature including marine life. The
red-tide that has been plaguing the shores is caused by the increase
in salt in the seawater pumped out by the desalination plants, this
does not only harm society in the long-term, but causes problems for
the UAE's image as a great tourist destination now.'

Concerning effects of the financial crisis: 'the crises meant that CSR
had to be put on the back burner since companies were struggling
to survive', but also 'the crisis seems to have had a cleansing effect.
Whereas before CSR was a lot of marketing and green washing as
part of the opportunistic boom, the efforts now are more genuinely
geared toward a better long-term future.' An Emirati interviewee
explained:

> CSR is introduced as a western concept. It does not translate well
> into Arabic. Courses offered are almost exclusively in English,
> which makes it more difficult for native Arabic speakers to

comprehend. Apart from the language we cannot relate to all concepts equally. We feel strongly about our religious duties of charity and caring for society.

On taboo topics:

There are still many taboo topics. HIV and drugs prevention are some, but most notably are human rights issues related to laborers. Things are changing, but they are changing slowly, the change will have to come from the Emirati population who have a stake in the long-term society, not expats who are looking to earn some money and leave.

The items unique to the region can be summarized in the model 'Drivers and Obstacles of CSR in the Middle East' (Figure 7.3).

Middle Eastern CSR reporting examples

Some organizations (CSR Arabia, Dubai Chamber of Commerce, the Pearl Initiative) organize events around CSR reporting, which indicates that efforts do develop CSR and its reporting are under way in the Middle East. To illustrate some CSR external reporting efforts from the GCC, we have chosen two indices, the Saudi

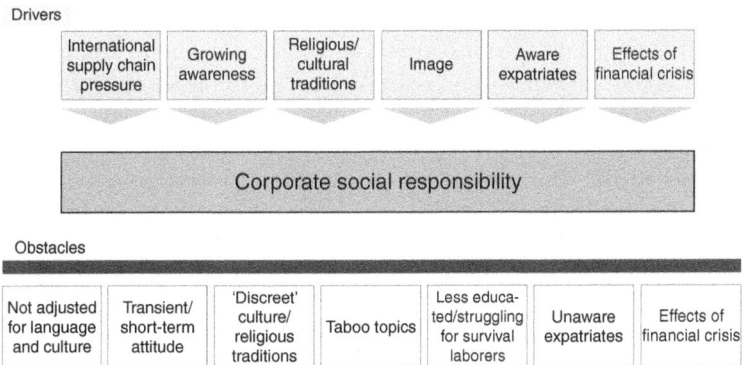

Figure 7.3 Drivers and Obstacles of CSR in the Middle East (Vinke and El-Khatib, 2011)
Source: Reproduced with the permission of Vinke and El-Khatib (2011).

Responsible Competitiveness Index and the S&P Hawkamah ESG Index, as positive examples.

The Saudi Responsible Competitiveness Index

Based on the belief that 'socially responsible business practices are an important building block of corporate and national development' ('The Saudi Responsible Competitiveness Index', 2008, p. 3), as well as the idea that CSR-based business models assist organizations in differentiating themselves from competitors, managing their risks and improving their internal functions, the Saudi Arabian General Investment Authority (SAGIA) has launched the Saudi Responsible Competitiveness Index ('The Saudi Responsible Competitiveness Index', 2008). This yearly index assesses, using globally recognized indicators, responsible development in Saudi Arabia. Responsible development refers to 'the leadership, policies, and practices that build sustainable development' ('The Saudi Responsible Competitiveness Index', 2008, p. 13). For each participating organization, the index assesses areas such as the organization's 'strategy, management, engagement processes, and performance systems' ('The Saudi Responsible Competitiveness Index', 2008, p. 24).

The indicators are then used to rank companies, the first three of which are recognized through the King Khalid Responsible Competitiveness Award (KKRCA). It is believed that rewarding leadership for CSR will encourage these firms to follow through with CSR and for other firms to follow suit. For the remaining organizations, a confidential report on 'performance against sector, national, and global benchmarks' as well as ways to improve responsible competitiveness will be provided ('The Saudi Responsible Competitiveness Index', 2008, p. 24). It is hoped that as time passes, more firms will participate in the index, enabling Saudi Arabia to develop a database of firms and their CSR-related practices. This can then be used to develop policies to strengthen CSR, which can be applied across businesses and used to make a difference to the corporate climate of the country as a whole.

The index is now in its third year, and while it rewards the top-performing organizations, it keeps the scores of the other participating organizations confidential ('Frequently Asked Questions', 2011). The index thus represents the Middle Eastern CSR model, as it is based on the pillars of the Middle Eastern culture, which is still not accustomed to full transparency. Hence, not only are the scores confidential, but so too are the results of the process of ranking the organizations as well as methods for improvement. The use of globally recognized indicators, however, proves that the core of CSR is the same regardless of culture. The point to conclude is that while the core features of CSR are applicable across cultures, the development of practically applicable CSR reporting practices will vary according to culture.

The S&P Hawkamah ESG index

Hawkamah is the 'corporate governance institute' and 'think tank' of the MENA region ('History', 2010). Based in the UAE, Hawkamah was developed in 2005 to aid the development of corporate governance practices in this region. As such, the institute assists the region's countries to 'develop...and implement...sound, well integrated corporate governance frameworks' ('Vision, Mission, and Values', 2010). The institute is a leader in driving CSR reporting in the region, focusing on the values of 'transparency, accountability, fairness, disclosure, and responsibility' ('Vision, Mission, and Values', 2010).

Toward that purpose, Hawkamah, in association with Standard & Poors (S&P) and with the support of the International Finance Corporation (IFC), has recently launched the MENA region's first 'Environmental, Social and Governance Index' ('ESG Index', 2010). Known as the S&P Hawkamah ESG index, it aims to 'raise the profile' of companies that adopt 'sustainable business practices' and reporting by providing comparable qualitative information on such companies in 'Saudi Arabia, the United Arab Emirates, Kuwait, Qatar, Bahrain, Oman, Jordan, Egypt, Lebanon, Morocco and Tunisia' ('ESG Index', 2010). The index will include listed companies from the above listed countries, which will be selected based on market capitalization, then analyzed and ranked ('ESG Index', 2010). These rankings are then disclosed to the public through 'annual reports, websites, bulletins, and disclosures made on stock exchanges' ('ESG Index', 2010). This transparency will help attract long-term institutional investors that would like to invest in socially responsible businesses in the region, eventually making the market less volatile ('ESG Index', 2010).

The S&P Hawkamah ESG Index is considered to be broader than the Saudi Responsible Competitiveness Index, given that it covers the entire MENA region. It is also considered to be more transparent, since the rankings are disclosed and become part of the public domain. It is the first attempt to compare and address the reporting problems of the region as a whole and, with time, it will help drive changes to CSR and its reporting in the region.

Conclusions and recommendations

CSR reporting has no doubt developed in the recent years, but there is still much more work to be done. The drivers and obstacles to CSR development presented above indicate that, at least for the UAE, there is a need to increase transparency when raising financing, to assess expected governmental drivers and to assess the impact of the increasing international supply chain pressure on the CSR practices of UAE corporations. We believe that such conclusions can also be drawn out for the entire Middle East region, despite the lack of a current examination of the drivers and hindrances in each of the region's countries. We think that focusing on these areas will bring about further developments in CSR reporting.

At the core of CSR development, however, is the need to raise awareness of CSR and CSR reporting in the region. While the examples presented in the chapter indicate that awareness does exist, it does so at the level of governments and formal authorities. Awareness of CSR and its reporting is still low in many organizations, particularly among SMEs, which constitute most of the home-grown businesses in the Middle East. As such, raising awareness will enable these firms to change the way they do business and report their activities internally and externally. This will help the adopting firms become sustainably profitable, and will aid the economic, social and environmental development of the Middle East region. Companies need to understand and develop CSR and help it mature and become more institutionalized. One element of this will be internal measurement and reporting, and external verifiable and accurate disclosure. Without this it will not be possible for CSR in the Middle East to move on to the next level.

Acknowledgments

We gratefully acknowledge the ongoing support of the ICAEW's Middle East office, which has provided funding for our research. We would also like to extend our sincere thanks to the numerous people that have shared their experience and insights, in particular the ICAEW's Regional Director Amanda Line and Head of Sustainability Richard Spencer, KMPG's Sustainability Partner Andrew Robinson, and Vineetha Mathew, Senior Executive CSR Training from the Dubai Chamber Centre for Responsible Business.

Notes

1. *Zakat* is one of the five pillars in Islam. It is regarded as a type of worship and self-purification (http://www.bbc.co.uk/religion/religions/islam/practices/zakat.shtml).
2. Unlike *Zakat*, which is an involuntary form of charity, *Sadqa* is a voluntary form of charity.

References

Aerts, W., & Cormier, D. (2009). Media legitimacy and corporate environmental communication. *Accounting, Organizations and Society, 34*(1), 1–27.

Al-Khater, K., & Naser, K. (2003). Users' perceptions of corporate social responsibility and accountability: Evidence from an emerging economy. *Managerial Auditing Journal, 18*(6/7), 538–548. doi: 10.1108/02686900310482678.

Boesso, G., & Michelon, G. (2010). The effects of stakeholder prioritization on corporate financial performance: An empirical investigation. *International Journal of Management, 27*(3), 470–496. Retrieved April 12, 2011, from ABI/INFORM Global. (Document ID: 2184287391.)

Brown, H. S., De Jong, M., & Levy, D. L. (2009). Building institutions based on information disclosure: Lessons from GRI's sustainability reporting. *Journal of Cleaner Production, 17 (6)*, 571–580. doi: 10.1016/j.jclepro.2008.12.009.

Burritt, R. L., & Schaltegger, S. (2010). Sustainability accounting and reporting: Fad or trend? *Accounting, Auditing & Accountability Journal, 23*(7), 829–846. doi: 10.1108/09513571011080144.

Dilling, P. F. A. (2010). Sustainability reporting in a global context : What are the characteristics of corporations that provide high quality sustainability reports – an empirical analysis. *International Business & Economics Research Journal, 9(1)*, 19–30.

ESG index (2010). Retrieved April 7, 2011, from Hawkamah website: http://www.hawkamah.org/sectors/esg/

Estidama Pearl Rating System (2010). Retrieved June 6, 2011, from Estidama website: http://estidama.org/estidama-and-pearl-rating-system.aspx?lang=en-US

Figge, F., Hahn, T., Schaltegger, S., & Wagner, M. (2002). The sustainability balanced scorecard – Linking sustainability management to business strategy. *Business Strategy and the Environment, 11*(5), 269–284. doi: 10.1002/bse.339.

Frequently Asked Questions (2011). Retrieved September 20, 2011, from Saudi Responsibility Competitiveness Index website: http://www.rci.org.sa/FAQ.html

Gray, R., Owen, D., & Adams, C. (2010). Some theories for social accounting?: A review essay and a tentative pedagogic categorisation of theorisations around social accounting. *Sustainability, Environmental Performance and Disclosures – Advances in Environmental Accounting & Management, 4*, 1–54. Retrieved September 20, 2011, from Emerald Database.

History (2010). Retrieved September 20, 2011, from Hawkamah website: http://www.hawkamah.org/about_hawkamah/history/index.html

Hopwood, A., Unerman, J., & Fries, J. (2010). *Accounting for sustainability: Practical insights.* London, UK: Earthscan Ltd.

ICAEW (2004). *Sustainability: The role of accountants.* Retrieved from Institute of Chartered Accountants in England and Wales website: http://www.icaew.com/~/media/Files/Technical/Financial-reporting/Information%20for%20better%20markets/IFBM/sustainability.ashx

KPMG International Survey of Corporate Responsibility Reporting (2005). KPMG Global Sustainability Services.

Mezher, T., Tabbara, S., & Al-Hosani, N. (2010). An overview of CSR in the renewable energy sector: Examples from the Masdar Initiative in Abu Dhabi. *Management of Environmental Quality: An International Journal, 21*(6), 744–760. doi: 10.1108/14777831011077619.

Rettab, B., Brik, A. B., & Mellahi, K. (2008). A study of management perceptions of the impact of corporate social responsibility on organisational performance in emerging economies: The case of Dubai. *Journal of Business Ethics, 89*(3), 371–390. doi: 10.1007/s10551-008-0005-9.

Reynolds, M., & Yuthas, K. (2008). Moral discourse and corporate social responsibility reporting. *Journal of Business Ethics, 78*(1–2), 47–64. doi: 10.1007/s10551-006-9316-x.

The SA8000 Standard (2010). Retrieved February 14, 2011, from Social Accountability International website: http://www.sa-intl.org/index.cfm?fuseaction=Page.ViewPage&PageID=937

The Saudi Responsible Competitiveness Index (2008). Retrieved September 20, 2011, from AccountAbility website: http://www.accountability.org/images/content/0/8/080/The%20Saudi%20Responsible%20Competitiveness%20Index_January.pdf

Scholtens, B. (2006). Finance as a driver of corporate social responsibility. *Journal of Business Ethics, 68*(1), 19-33. doi: 10.1007/s10551-006-9037-1.

Snider, J., Hill, R. P., & Martin, D. (2003). Corporate social responsibility in the 21st century: A view from the world's most successful firms. *Journal of Business Ethics, 48*(2), 175–187. doi: 10.1023/B:BUSI.0000004606.29523.db.

Summary (2011). Retrieved February 14, 2011, from the European Commission – Environment website: http://ec.europa.eu/environment/emas/about/summary_en.htm

Sustainability Decision-Making Model (2010). Retrieved April 8, 2011, from Accounting for Sustainability website: http://www.accountingforsustainability.org/files/pdf/Decision%20Making%20Tutorial%20-%20pdf[1].pdf

Thurm, R. (2006). Taking the GRI to scale: Towards the next generation of sustainability reporting guidelines. *Sustainability Accounting and Reporting*, 325–337. doi: 10.1007/978-1-4020-4974-3_14.

Vision, Mission, and Values (2010). Retrieved September 20, 2011, from Hawkamah website: http://www.hawkamah.org/about_hawkamah/vision_mission_values/index.html

Visser, W., Matten, D., Pohl, M., & Tolhurst, N. (2010). *The A to Z of corporate social responsibility*. West Sussex, UK: John Wiley & Sons Ltd.

Vogel, D. (2005). *The market for virtue: The potential and limits of corporate social responsibility*. Washington, DC: The Brookings Institution.

What Are the G3 Guidelines (2011). Retrieved September 20, 2011, from Global Reporting Initiative website: http://www.globalreporting.org/reportingframework/g3guidelines

What Is GRI (2011). Retrieved September 20, 2011, from Global Reporting Initiative website: http://www.globalreporting.org/AboutGRI/WhatIsGRI/

8
The AUB Neighborhood Initiative: Social Responsibility in a University's Backyard

Tonnie Choueiri and Cynthia Myntti

Introduction

Some might find it surprising to see a chapter about a university in a book on corporate social responsibility (CSR). However, like businesses, many universities are now asking how they can be more socially responsible 'citizens' of their communities. Many of the same forces are at work in businesses and at universities to encourage new thinking and action on social responsibility, ranging from the basic utilitarian pressures to generate good publicity to the realignment of core business practices and relationships around clearly articulated ethical principles.

A cross-fertilization of ideas has occurred between the academic and business worlds. The growth of CSR worldwide has encouraged organizations of many types, including universities, to look within and reinforce or renew their own social practices (Leitão and Silva, 2007). So too the CSR discourse elaborated on by academics, such as those contributing to this current volume, has encouraged, even provoked, business leaders to consider explicitly the variety of CSR approaches they might adopt.

This chapter begins with a review of the literature on the social responsibility of universities. While much of this literature is North American, many of the contradictions and challenges faced by universities there will resonate in the Middle East. The chapter then presents the case of the Neighborhood Initiative at the American University of Beirut, which seeks to share the university's intellectual resources for the public good in the district of Beirut just outside the campus walls. The case of the Neighborhood Initiative most closely mirrors what is called 'strategic CSR', and it highlights the issues that arise when adopting this approach to community engagement. The chapter then examines CSR through some new writing on social responsibility and place-making, and ends with some observations that can serve as reminders to both academic and business organizations.

The social responsibility of universities

Many of the world's oldest and most prestigious institutions of higher learning have been known for their other-worldliness, removed and isolated from the hustle and bustle of everyday life, 'ivory towers' where scholarly activities are carried out undisturbed (Bok, 1982). Since the mid-19th century, however, universities have increasingly been challenged to become engaged, relevant and useful for solving their societies' most pressing problems. As early as 1862, the land-grant colleges in the USA were created to contribute explicitly to the social and economic welfare of rural USA (Axelroth and Dubb, 2010, p. 19; Howard and Alperovitz, 2010, p. ix). Since the 1960s, calls have increased to apply the same ideas to urban areas (Berdahl et al., 2011).

By their very mission, universities advance knowledge and provide new generations with an education that equips them for a productive life and prepares them to become active citizens in their societies and in the world. Universities alone can grant the degrees needed for certain careers, and their faculties possess exclusive knowledge based on years of research and reflection. From this privileged position comes responsibility. In a seminal work on the subject of universities' social responsibility, Derek Bok, then president of Harvard University, made the case that, given their noble mission to advance society through knowledge production, universities have a duty to use their resources to respond to public needs (Bok, 1982, pp. 62–78).

Indeed, all three 'pillars' of academia – teaching, research and service – can be socially responsive and responsible. Many university campuses now promote service-learning, which refers to the mutual and experiential learning that occurs when students engage in volunteer or community work, benefiting the organizations or communities in which they serve and getting experience they could not gain in classroom settings (Furco, 1996, p. 9). It is now possible to find more references to 'engaged scholarship', with special encouragement of community-based research directed at solving pressing societal problems (Harkavy et al., 2009, p. 151; Howard and Alperovitz, 2010, p. ix). And service can help to ensure that 'the work of the academy (relates) to the world beyond the campus' (Boyer, 1990, p. 75; Silka, 1999, p. 336). Reflecting on the service imperative, former Brazilian minister of culture, poet and singer Gilberto Gil has stated, 'Universities, beyond an educational role for increasing knowledge, assume a civic role for disseminating values. In that case, the most important human value is solidarity' (Leitão and Silva, 2007, p. 6–7, 10).

Universities also model socially responsible behavior by how they conduct the business side of their operations. An institution's policies and procedures on a wide range of activities – from hiring practices, working conditions and purchasing preferences, to public transport subsidies for employees and campus recycling and energy conservation – reflect its fundamental values (Axelroth and Dubb, 2010, p. 28). The University of Pennsylvania, for instance, created an 'economic inclusion' program so that its purchasing of goods and services could more explicitly benefit businesses in the disadvantaged area of Philadelphia where the university is located (Rodin, 2007, p. 130). Internationally, the Talloires global network of 200 universities and the COPERNICUS program of more than 300 European universities have committed signatory institutions to follow new and exemplary practices in environmental sustainability, among other practices (Leitão and Silva, 2007, p. 7; The Talloires Network, 2011).

Urban universities face particular problems that demand solutions. In the USA, for example, the decline of the old manufacturing centers in the north and north-east has led to urban poverty and decay around long-established universities. For these institutions, their very survival as a place attractive to excellent faculty staff and students requires urgent engagement and problem-solving with their urban environment. In other urban settings, universities are witnesses, and even inadvertent contributors, to gentrification, densification, congestion and other urban problems (Axelroth and Dubb, 2010, p. 2).

The literature on a specific strain of socially responsible actions – university–community partnerships – identifies five main challenges that arise when universities choose to be socially responsible urban neighbors. First, problem-solving requires collaboration; and within the university itself it almost always requires interdisciplinary collaboration. Although many academic leaders praise interdisciplinarity, too few incentives exist to overcome the barriers to such work. Urban problem-solving also requires collaboration between the university and its neighbors, and among actors in the neighborhood, such as businesses, non-profit organizations and residents. The experience of university–community collaborations in North America suggests that both sides must collaborate well internally in order to collaborate well together (Axelroth and Dubb, 2010, p. 36). Similarly, this experience shows that university–community collaborations can lead to a restructuring of both the universities and the communities. And finally, while collaborations can be difficult, they have the capacity to expand the resources available and to bring about results that could not be achieved by either party on its own, or by other types of agencies (Silka, 1999, pp. 335–338).

The second challenge is priority setting. The key questions are: whose priorities count, and how are they determined? Often universities act without any substantial consultation and according to their own priorities: setting up practice sites for students, facilitating campus expansion, or increasing the safety of neighborhood streets to protect their students (Maurrasse, 2001; Rodin, 2007). Durable relationships, however, cannot begin with an agenda imposed by the university, or indeed by any particularly powerful constituency in the neighborhood. Urban neighborhoods are socially complex, rarely a homogeneous 'community', and do not hold one view of what is important to address first. Local needs and priorities must therefore be identified, paying meticulous attention to the process through which they are arrived at (Axelroth and Dubb, 2010, p. 35). But collaborative priority setting is not easy. The University of Pennsylvania's West Philadelphia Initiatives stayed away from public meetings and community visioning sessions to define the university's priorities; they felt that this approach tends to raise expectations and create problems in collaborative relations between the university and its neighbors. Instead, the University of Pennsylvania let multiple interactions on multiple fronts suggest which issues were of greatest concern to both and how to go about responding (Rodin, 2007, p. 20).

The third, and related, challenge to universities wanting to help solve the problems of their urban environments is to find the intersection between the interests of the university faculty and neighbors' needs and aspirations. The faculty is the intellectual soul of the institution, and it has the expertise needed for local problem-solving. The greatest force is created when this intersection is found. For example, imagine that neighbors of an urban university become angry and frustrated by traffic-related congestion in their streets, much of it caused by the cars of university students, staff and visitors. At the same time, the engineering faculty of the university has internationally recognized expertise in traffic planning. A university–neighborhood initiative to address neighborhood congestion promises to be a win-win venture. Derek Bok observes that when initiatives are at this intersection of interests, they garner the most support and create the most value (Bok, 1982, p. 77).

The fourth challenge relates to power disparities evident when a powerful university works with unorganized, disempowered neighbors (Myntti et al., forthcoming, p. 16). Ideally, universities should engage all their resources in 'democratic, mutually beneficial, mutually respectful partnerships' with their communities and to adapt their work and resources for the public good (Harkavy et al., 2009, pp. 149–151). The literature contains many illustrations of the opposite, where universities take advantage of their comparatively powerful position vis-à-vis their neighbors to pursue their own interests. A related problem is one of perceptions; neighbors often perceive the university to have a bottomless bank account to respond to community needs. In both instances, real partnerships can only emerge when the more powerful party takes care to listen and not to impose, and when trust and working relationships are built up over time (Adams, 2003, p. 573; Axelroth and Dubb, 2010, p. 36). Ensuring an authentically participatory collaboration is a constant effort, but community buy-in and trust, as well as clear ongoing communication, are essential (Axelroth and Dubb, 2010, p. 39).

The fifth and final challenge is adequate institutional support for neighborhood problem-solving. Universities have to ensure that they have the internal institutional set-up that supports collaborations most, and assists in making things happen. A commitment to social progress is not simply an external pursuit; to bring about the most change, all the university's resources must be involved: human, academic, cultural and economic (Harkavy et al., 2009, p. 147; Howard and Alperovitz, 2010, p. x), and adjustments made to its organizational culture, structures, policies and day-to-day activities (Harkavy et al., 2009, p. 149). Having a centralized unit for outreach facilitates collaboration and coordination. It is also essential to have the practical, not just rhetorical, support of the administration. Presidents and deans set priorities. They can encourage problem-focused community based research by providing funding and other incentives. But to be sustainable over the long term, support must become institutionalized so that it persists despite changes of administration (Bok, 1982, p. 86; Axelroth and Dubb, 2010, p. 36) (Figure 8.1).

Despite these considerable challenges, the literature on the social role of urban universities in North America suggests that they can and do have a substantial positive influence on their neighborhoods and cities. Universities and their affiliated medical centers (the so-called 'Eds and Meds') are place-based institutions with local, and often regional and national, influence (Harkavy et al., 2009, p. 151; Axelroth and Dubb, 2010, p. 34). In a report to the US Department of Housing and Urban Development, Harkavy et al. (2009) argue that 'Eds and Meds' are vital for revitalizing US cities and communities. Their mission and economic interests compel them to care about their communities, and they have the resources to bring about change (Harkavy et al., 2009, pp. 147–148). University administrators are increasingly appreciating that the long-term strength of their institutions is inseparably connected to the stability of surrounding neighborhoods (Howard and Alperovitz, 2010, p. ix). Harkavy et al. propose that if government and universities pursue engagement

Challenges to university-community partnerships
1. **Facilitating internal and external collaboration** *(between departments in the university, between the university and the community, and among community actors themselves)*
2. **Setting priorities** *(whose priorities to choose, and how to identify community needs)*
3. **Identifying the intersection between faculty interests and community concerns and aspirations**
4. **Ensuring an authentically participatory process**
5. **Cultivating real institutional support beyond rhetoric** *(all university resources must be involved, and structures may have to be adjusted)*

Figure 8.1 Challenges to University–Community Partnerships

with cities correctly, the results could include an improvement in the quality of life of urban dwellers and of learning, an increase in the competitiveness of cities, and even a more democratic and just society (Harkavy et al., 2009, p. 150).

The AUB Neighborhood Initiative

The American University of Beirut (AUB) was established in 1866 as the Syrian Protestant College on a campus far outside the walls of the city. In the succeeding century and a half, the city of Beirut enveloped AUB. By the mid-20th century, the neighborhood surrounding AUB was the city's most glamorous and modern, combining a mix of uses: residential, commercial, retail, educational and entertainment. The Lebanese Civil War (1975–1990) created physical destruction and social upheaval everywhere, and AUB's neighborhood was not immune to these negative forces. Even now, a nagging juxtaposition exists between AUB's serene park-like campus and the congested and run-down urban districts that surround it (Myntti, 2009).

Administratively, the districts of Ras Beirut and Ain Mreisseh that abut the university are 2 of 12 such districts in municipal Beirut. The population of municipal Beirut as a whole is estimated at nearly half a million, which represents a quarter of the population of greater Beirut (CAS, 2009). The districts surrounding AUB are, on average, better educated than Beirut as a whole, have fewer families with children and a higher proportion of older and one-person house-holds. A recently conducted survey, however, suggests that pockets of poverty and ill health exist next to affluence (Kaddour et al., 2011).

The AUB Neighborhood Initiative was launched in 2007 to address the problems of the city just outside its walls, including: congestion, crumbling infrastructure, densification, a lack of greenery and pub-lic space, gentrification, a lack of affordable housing and growing income disparities.

In reaching out to Ras Beirut, the Neighborhood Initiative builds on a long tradition of community engagement and service. From its earliest days, AUB's missionary founders inculcated the value of service in the institution, and soon the university and its students were providing medical care to the needy, education to the local population and humanitarian assistance during war, famines and other crises. From the 1930s, as Arab nationalism swept through the region, AUB faculty and students were at the forefront of the push for secular national development, embarking on rural development, agricultural modernization programs and much more. This work moved from being conceived of as voluntary and extracurricular to a central dimension of student coursework and faculty research. During the civil war and in subsequent crises, AUB contributed heroically through its emergency medical services, public-health investigations, relief efforts for displaced persons and the reconstruction of damaged communities (Myntti et al., 2009, pp. 8–20; Axelroth and Dubb, 2010, p. 34).

The Neighborhood Initiative thus draws on a long institutional history of outreach, and an academic mission of civic and social responsibility. The current AUB Mission Statement contains clear reference to social engagement:

> Graduates will be individuals committed to creative and critical thinking, life-long learning, personal integrity and civic responsibility, and leadership.

The aim of the Neighborhood Initiative is to mobilize university resources, primarily its unique intellectual resources, for the public good of the neighborhood. But this is not a one-way flow of good works; the Neighborhood Initiative conceives that it being a socially responsible urban institution is mutually beneficial. AUB will increase its attractiveness to excellent faculty staff and students if its neighborhood, its place in the city, is attractive: lively, livable and affordable. And AUB's teaching and research will be enriched and made more relevant by addressing the real-world problems confronting its neighbors in Ras Beirut. In a word, the Neighborhood Initiative recognizes that one of AUB's greatest comparative advantages is its location in Ras Beirut, and also that its relationships to its place cannot be treated merely as background – they must be nurtured and ever invigorated.

The Neighborhood Initiative is located in the office of the university's president, which gives it visibility and authority to work across the university's many academic and business units. With a small staff of two, the Neighborhood Initiative does not itself conduct projects. Rather, it plays a support role to faculty and student-led projects and often collaborates with a sister initiative, AUB's newly established Center for Civic Engagement and Community Service

(CCECS). CCECS promotes service-learning and community-based volunteerism and research at AUB, with an academic emphasis but not a geographic focus. The Neighborhood Initiative has a specific place-making emphasis, and works with both academic and non-academic units, such as facilities, housing, business-services and security.

The research and outreach activities supported by the Neighborhood Initiative may be broadly categorized as improving the urban environment, enhancing community and well-being and protecting the diversity of Ras Beirut. The following are examples of ongoing projects:

Improving the urban environment

- The Neighborhood Congestion Studies respond to the problems of congestion and the conflict between pedestrians and cars at the southern edge of campus. Led by a multidisciplinary team of traffic engineers, urban designers and a social scientist, the project has involved a variety of stakeholders to develop its recommendations for action. Work to date has recommended widening sidewalks and creating drop-off zones, among other interventions. Current research is investigating parking options and the creation of a shared semi-public transportation system to serve the area.
- The Inclusive Neighborhood project brings together the CCECS, landscape design students and the social science faculty to address neighbors' complaints about the poor walkability of Ras Beirut's streets and sidewalks. It proposes a redesign of Jeanne d'Arc Street, a main neighborhood artery, into a model street that is accessible to all, including those with wheelchairs or strollers, serving as an example for the rest of the city.
- Greening the Neighborhood responds to concerns about the lack of green spaces, and is being tackled by civil and environmental engineering students and the landscape design department. They have designed rainwater catchment systems and roof gardens, to be placed on various residential and institutional roofs; the only solution in light of the absence of empty lots.

All three of these projects will move into challenging implementation phases in the coming year.

Enhancing community and well-being

- The Ras Beirut Well-Being Survey, a participatory social, economic and demographic survey of neighborhood households, addresses the lack of current information about the well-being of the population of Ras Beirut. The multidisciplinary research team, from public health, sociology, anthropology and economics, engaged neighbors at every stage of the research. Public presentations held at different locations in Hamra shared the findings and solicited feedback on possible interventions.
- The University for Seniors (جامعة الكبار) responds to the aspirations of older neighbors to stay intellectually challenged and socially engaged. Older people can become members of the University for Seniors, contribute to its governance and lead most activities, such as study groups, public lectures and educational trips.

Protecting the diversity of Ras Beirut

- The Neighborhood Initiative is represented on the president's Housing Task Force, and actively contributes to the Housing Strategy Study. Investing in affordable housing in the neighborhood is a major plank in the evolving AUB housing strategy.

Each of these projects is the result of, and developed through, the Neighborhood Initiative's broad and multifaceted facilitation. This facilitation begins with continuous, mostly informal, contact with a wide variety of neighbors to keep a 'finger on the pulse' and understand their most important concerns. Unlike the university neighborhoods written about in North American literature, Ras Beirut does not have community development organizations or representative neighborhood groups that the university might reach out to and work with. So the process of engagement involves painstaking and systematic contact with individual businesses, residents, local government officials and leaders of the neighborhood's religious institutions.

Second, the Neighborhood Initiative keeps abreast of faculty and student interests. It is crucial to know where in the university to find the relevant expertise for addressing local problems, and to ascertain which faculty and students would be willing to devote their energy to Ras Beirut issues. AUB could never address every problem in the neighborhood, but finding the crucial intersection of concern, expertise and interest provides a focus.

Third, the Neighborhood Initiative, with a grant from an international foundation, provides seed funding to new activities. In this sense, one of its roles is that of catalyst for activities on and with the neighborhood. These funds typically support modest research costs, research assistants, meeting refreshments and communication materials. And although modest, they make a difference by encouraging a neighborhood focus and a respectful, participatory approach.

Fourth, the Neighborhood Initiative advocates for the neighborhood in high-level policy reform at AUB. For example, the university is in the process of revising its support to the faculty for housing. The Neighborhood Initiative has encouraged the university leadership to employ innovative strategies for providing more affordable housing in Ras Beirut. The neighborhood is gentrifying; that is, its character is changing through the demolition of run-down residential buildings, the displacement of long-time residents and the construction of new luxury towers catering to a global financial elite. By investing in real estate to increase the supply of affordable housing in Ras Beirut, the university would be responding to the needs of its faculty and at the same time helping to protect the economic diversity of the neighborhood. This is a perfect example of a mutually beneficial, or win-win, approach.

Fifth, recognizing that the faculty and students have many other pressing commitments and limited time to give to neighborhood work, the Neighborhood Initiative provides them with various forms of logistical support. These range from making introductions, keeping meeting minutes, writing needed correspondence, securing required permissions, producing copies, researching further funding options, organizing consultations with residents, businesses, developers and government officials, and, when the time comes, strategizing about implementation and facilitating the desired changes. Because the faculty is not used to dealing with implementation issues, and because of the problematic nature of public jurisdiction in Lebanon, the help provided by the Neighborhood Initiative is vital (Myntti et al., 2009, p. 24) (Figure 8.2).

Taken together, the roles played by the Neighborhood Initiative facilitate the connections between the university and its neighbors, between the 'town and gown', and make things happen. Writing

The AUB Neighborhood Initiative:
1. Stays informed of neighborhood needs and aspirations through continuous informal contact
2. Keeps abreast of the interests and expertise of faculty and students
3. Provides seed funding for new neighborhood-targeted projects and activities
4. Advocates for the neighborhood in high-level policy forums in the university
5. Provides diverse logistical support (anything needed) to teams of busy faculty and students

Figure 8.2   The AUB Neighborhood Initiative

about these functions in the North American context, Reardon (2006) noted how critical the need was for 'boundary crossers'; universities that do not create the institutional space and offer support for boundary crossers can expect to have a limited effect on their neighborhoods.

As the Neighborhood Initiative passes its fourth birthday and looks to the future, some lessons from the literature on strategic CSR are worth applying at AUB regarding its work with its neighborhood. Prime among them is recognizing the ways in which a social responsibility agenda can and should shape the way an organization operates, from corporate culture to daily operations (Heslin and Ochoa, 2008, p. 129). For example, how can AUB promote environmental responsibility and accessibility in its neighborhood if it does not follow these norms itself? Similarly, strategic CSR warns organizations to be focused, to harness the power of their institutional type (Porter and Kramer, 2011, p. 64). Businesses are businesses, not charities, and universities are neither charities nor governments. The lesson is: choose projects carefully and do not attempt to perform roles that should be filled by others. Finally, strategic CSR encourages companies to take a long-term view of success, not focus on short-term costs, and get out ahead of industry trends and regulations (Heslin and Ochoa, 2008, p. 126; Porter and Kramer, 2011, pp. 64–69). Recognizing that AUB currently has few regional peers in its neighborhood-focused outreach is a reminder that both validates and further challenges the Neighborhood Initiative.

CSR and place-making

A recent addition to the CSR literature examines the role of institutions in place-making. This has particular relevance to the analysis of the AUB Neighborhood Initiative in this volume, as the initiative's center of attention, and its strength, is its local focus, and we believe this can be an inspiration to companies. Locations have traditionally been viewed by companies and by management literature as 'backdrops' for corporate operations (Thomas and Cross, 2007, p. 33). Today, just as universities are increasingly looking out into, and engaging with, their neighborhoods, companies stand to benefit from including a local perspective in their social responsibility practices. According to Thomas and Cross (2007), 'place' is composed of three realms: the material, the natural and the social. The material realm refers to the built environment and the economy; the natural realm refers to the natural environment; and the social realm refers to the full spectrum of human interactions and the patterns that shape the relationships between individuals and institutions. They propose a definition of CSR 'that defines corporations as agents, whose actions, values, behaviors, and strategies contribute in myriad ways to the social construction of places'. They theorize about the impact of organizational strategies and behaviors on the places in which corporations are located, and suggest that this lens could facilitate a comprehensive evaluation of CSR activities undertaken (pp. 34–35).

Thomas and Cross have developed a provocative typology of organizations and their relationship to place. Two viewpoints exist, which reveal not only how corporations see themselves in relation to place but also 'the meaning they give to place, which then influences their goals, contributions to place, and all variety of behavior'. One viewpoint conceptualizes corporations and their success as interdependent with the well-being of place; the other conceptualizes corporations and their success as independent of place. Organizations of the first type consider themselves as responsible for the material, natural and social realms of place; view their success as intimately tied to the greater well-being of place; and proactively seek opportunities to invest in their place. Organizations of the second type, on the other hand, see themselves primarily as economic agents and occupants of place. Their primary responsibility is to their shareholders, not to the places in which they are located, and generating jobs and tax revenues is their main contribution to place. As a result, they may ignore the social and natural resources of their place, often to their own long-term detriment (p. 40).

The following table elaborates this typology by categorizing organizations into four different approaches to place, how they conceptualize themselves as agents and then what this means for corporate behaviors and strategies (Thomas and Cross, 2007, pp. 41–42) (Table 8.1).

Thomas and Cross (2007) push the differences between these four to the extreme of caricature, but the contrasts are nonetheless revealing. Transformational organizations see themselves as change agents in their communities, and responsible for their well-being. Their organizational culture emphasizes collaboration, mutual learning, openness to change and building partnerships. Their policies and practices protect the environment, neighborhoods, cultural heritage, local economy and other local resources. They are often ahead of industry trends and regulation, and their actions are not solely aimed at public relations. At the other end of the spectrum, exploitative organizations value place for the resources – economic, social, cultural and political – that it can provide. Their mission is to maximize profit, and they are likely to leave a place once the return is not as lucrative as anticipated (pp. 45, 51).

Universities, like corporations, can also view themselves and their futures as either interdependent with, or independent of, their surrounding neighborhoods (Axelroth and Dubb, 2010, p. 34). As AUB expands and deepens its connections to Ras Beirut through its Neighborhood Initiative, it is useful and indeed inspiring to aim to be a transformational agent. This is the ultimate hope of a socially responsible institution.

Conclusion

Socially responsible universities and companies can have a powerful, positive impact on the places where they are located. Both have particular strengths and resources that are vital for tackling today's problems. And they can learn from each other.

Corporations can learn several important lessons on social responsibility from the discourse of universities. Perhaps the most important lesson has to do with how thematic priorities are set. The literature on university–community partnerships suggests that the strongest and most durable of them emerge out of a process of listening rather than imposing. At AUB, for instance, the Neighborhood Initiative has taken great care to take note of the concerns of neighbors, set its priorities accordingly, and then identify university talent to respond. The greatest challenge, and greatest potential synergy, comes from

172

Table 8.1 Organizations as Place Builders

	Place agent identity	Value of place	Cultural characteristics	Behavior	Strategy
Transformational	Change agents	Cultural and environmental entity, interdependent systems	Team-focused, collaboratively minded, values shared learning	Invest cultural and economic resources towards the well-being of place	To orchestrate organizational and place well-being, community collaboration
Contributive	Investors, contributors	Social network, resource	Community supporters, philanthropic/benevolent, paternalistic	Give to place via fundraising, sponsorship, and leadership without a specific accounting of how it benefits the organization	To participate in achieving place goals that build social and cultural capital which are consistent with the organizational mission
Contingent	Participants	Social, geographic, and economic commodity	Competitive, instrumental	Instrumental giving to place is based on specific and identifiable benefit to organization	To participate in achieving place activities/events that satisfy an organization's investment
Exploitative	Independent agents, industry-centric	Social, geographic, and economic commodity	Profit-oriented, manipulative, arrogant, ignorance	Exploit environmental, human, and cultural capital for corporate profit, limited giving (financial & volunteerism to local organizations	To achieve organizational goals at the expense of place

Source: Thomas and Cross (2007, p. 42).

finding the intersection between the concerns of neighbors and the passion and expertise of AUB faculty and students. The experience of universities also underscores the importance of committed leadership at the highest levels of the institution, and the need for both rhetorical and sufficient practical support for socially responsible projects.

Universities also have much to learn from socially responsible corporations, particularly in the area of strategic institutional benefit. For companies, the mutual benefit principle means much more than the immediate 'bottom line'. It is about a realignment of mission and operations, a clarification of ethical principles, and creating new ways of working that encourage innovation and creativity. The improved bottom line follows. Although non-profit institutions such as AUB do not consider the 'bottom line' in the same way that companies do, powerful parallels do still exist. The Neighborhood Initiative has learned that its activities are not just about 'doing good' for Ras Beirut, but rather about being good for the neighborhood *and* good for the university. By reaching out to the neighborhood, AUB strengthens its core academic mission by increasing the relevance of research and teaching. Students have the opportunity to develop innovative projects and theses, ones that win awards and resonate with prospective employers. The faculty gains new knowledge and local examples for use in teaching and in publications.

Finally, the well-being of universities and companies is connected to the well-being of their places. From a purely pragmatic point of view, place affects the availability of talent at present and in the future. Creative, skilled employees, world-class faculty staff and smart students are attracted by a high quality of life in a healthy and vibrant neighborhood. This chapter suggests that if an organization sees itself as a change agent in its community, and creates an organizational culture emphasizing collaboration, mutual learning and openness to change and building partnerships, their outreach will have concrete and visible effects on the environment, neighborhoods, cultural heritage, local economy and other local resources.

References

Adams, C. (2003). 'The Meds and Eds In Urban Economic Development', *Journal Of Urban Affairs*, 25, 5, 571–588.

Axelroth R. and Dubb, S. (2010). 'The Road Half Traveled: University Engagement at a Crossroads', *The Democracy Collaborative*, University of Maryland, December 2010.

Berdahl, R. M, Cohon, J. L., Simmons R. J., Sexton, J., and Berlowitz, L. C. (2011). 'The University and the City', *Bulletin of the American Academy*, Spring, 4–18.

Bok, D. (1982). *Beyond the Ivory Tower: Social Responsibilities of the Modern University*. Cambridge: Harvard University Press.

Boyer, E. L. (1990). *Scholarship Reconsidered: Priorities of the Professoriate*. New York: The Carnegie Foundation for the Advancement of Teaching.

Central Administration of Statistics (CAS), Republic of Lebanon (2009). 'Population Characteristics in 2009.' Unpublished report. Available: http://www.cas.gov.lb/index.php?option=com_content&view=article&id=113&Itemid=2=article&id=113&Itemid=63 (Accessed December 10, 2011).

Furco, A. (1996). 'Service-Learning: A Balanced Approach to Experiential Education', *Expanding Boundaries: Service and Learning*, Washington DC: Corporation for National Service. Reprinted in Campus Compact's (2000). *Introduction to Service Learning Toolkit*, 9–18.

Harkavy, I., Chair, et al. (2009). 'Anchor Institutions as Partners in Building Successful Communities and Local Economies' in Brophy, P. and Godsil, R. (eds) *Retooling HUD for a Catalytic Federal Government: A Report to Secretary Shaun Donovan*. Philadelphia, PA: Penn Institute for Urban Research, University of Pennsylvania, April 2009. http://penniur.upenn.edu/uploads/media_items/retooling-hud-report.original.pdf

Heslin, P. and Ochoa, J. (2008). 'Understanding and Developing Strategic Corporate Social Responsibility', *Organizational Dynamics*, 37, 125–144.

Howard, T. and Alperovitz, G. (2010). 'Preface' in Axelroth, R. and Dubb, S. (eds) *The Road Half Traveled: University Engagement at a Crossroads*, *The Democracy Collaborative*, University of Maryland, December 2010.

Kaddour, A., Zurayk, H., Salti, N., Abdulrahim, S., Wick, L. and Myntti, C. (2011). 'The Ras Beirut Well-Being Survey: Preliminary Results', unpublished posters.

Leitão, J. and Silva, M. J. (2007). 'CSR and Social Marketing: What is the Desired Role for Universities in Fostering Public Policies?' MPRA Paper No. 2954. Available: http://mpra.ub.uni-muenchen.de/2954/1/MPRA_paper_2954.pdf (Accessed August 14, 2011).

Maurrasse, D. (2001). *Beyond the Campus: How Colleges and Universities Form Partnerships with their Communities*. New York: Routledge.

Myntti, C. (2009). 'The American University of Beirut's Neighborhood Initiative', *Urban Land Middle East*, Spring, 71–73.

Myntti, C., Mabsout, M. and Zurayk, R. (forthcoming). 'Through Thick and Thin: The American University of Beirut Engages its Communities' in McIlrath, L., Lyons, A. and Munck, R. (eds) *Higher Education and Civic Engagement: Comparative Perspectives*. London: Palgrave, pp. 1–21.

Myntti, C., Zurayk, R. and Mabsout, M. (2009). 'Beyond the Walls: The American University of Beirut Engages its Communities', *Voices on*

Arab Philanthropy and Civic Engagement, Working paper number 3, John D. Gerhart Center, American University in Cairo.

Porter, M. and Kramer, M. (2011). 'Creating Shared Value', *Harvard Business Review*, 89, 1/2, 62–77.

Reardon, K. (2006). 'Promoting Reciprocity within Community/University Development Partnerships: Lessons from the Field', *Planning, Practice and Research*, 21, 1, 95–107.

Rodin, J. (2007). *The University and Urban Revival: Out of the Ivory Tower and Into the Streets*. Philadelphia: University of Pennsylvania Press.

Silka, L. (1999). 'Paradoxes of Partnerships: Reflections on University-Community Collaborations', *Research in Politics and Society*, 7, 335–359.

The Talloires Network (2007). 'What is the Talloires Network?' *Tufts University Website*. Available: http://www.tufts.edu/talloiresnetwork/?pid= 35 (Accessed September 20, 2011).

Thomas, D. F. and Cross, J. E. (2007). 'Organizations as Place Builders', *Journal of Behavioral and Applied Management*, September, 9, 1, 33–61.

Conclusions and the Future

Dima Jamali

This book offers an interesting selection of readings that deepen our understanding of CSR in the Middle East region. Through an assorted selection of coverage, examples and cases, it ponders the multiple facets of CSR in the region, including philanthropy; strategic giving; social entrepreneurship; internal CSR and responsible HR management practices; effective CSR integration in SMEs; CER and its evolution; CSR reporting and lingering challenges in this respect; as well as the relevance and applicability of CSR and corporate citizenship to a wider spectrum of societal actors and institutions. The various contributions have also nicely captured and reiterated the commitment to CSR in the Middle East, and the need for partnerships and joint initiatives that collectively build human capacity and strengthen the fabric of the social community. In essence, the future bodes well for CSR in the Middle East, and the common challenge we face is to shift to more organized forms of giving that leverage the strong traditions of philanthropy in the region but also channel them more effectively to address critical social needs, and meet the daunting challenge of sustainable development.

Index

177